LAUNCH
YOUR
PLATFORM

LAUNCH YOUR PLATFORM

A 21-day launch plan to build your personal brand and share your story online as a writer, coach, or speaker

Jonathan Milligan

Book Cover by Platform Growth Books

Illustrations by Jonathan Milligan

1st edition 2024

YOUR FREE GIFT

As a way of saying thanks for your purchase, we are offering a free companion online course called *The Launch Your Platform Accelerator Course.*

With this companion online course, you'll be able to fully implement all the exercises, worksheets, and checklists inside this book. To get free instant access, go to:

MarketYourMessage.com/Launch-Course

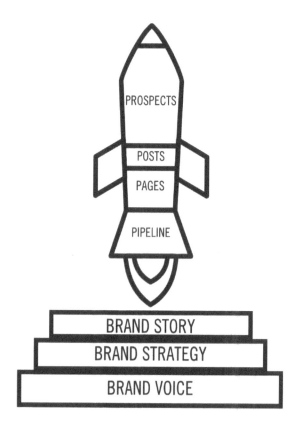

The Messenger Launch Plan

Inside the pages of this book, you'll discover a powerful framework known as the Messenger Launch Plan. To successfully launch your online business, you'll need to nail down your brand voice, brand strategy, and brand story.

Contents

Introduction

Your message deserves to be heard.

Yet, you may feel overwhelmed by the process of building an online platform. I've been there too. When I first started on this journey, I was flooded with questions about technology, marketing, and even my own expertise. As an insecure high school teacher, I never imagined having a platform to impact lives. The mere thought of public speaking made me queasy. Writing vulnerable stories for anyone beyond my journal felt uncomfortable.

After discovering my passion and message, everything changed. What began as a small blog sparked meaningful connections worldwide. Before I knew it, I was leading workshops and authoring books to amplify my message. The journey to owning my voice and embracing my destiny as a thought leader had messy moments. I share many of them in the coming pages.

I wrote this book to offer you the guiding hand I desperately wished for in my own humble beginnings. I'd love to have your permission to be your guide. I'll show you the exact steps to rise above the noise and get your message heard. I'm honored to walk this path of courage and change beside you.

Together, we'll go from finding your purpose to launching your online platform. You'll discover how to attract your tribe online.

You'll also learn how to forge real partnerships. Most importantly, you'll break through inner barriers holding you back from sharing your message.

If you feel even the slightest tug toward impacting others, this book provides the blueprint. Lay aside hesitation or perfectionism for now. Simply turn the page with an open mind and heart. We'll walk the path together step-by-step over the next 21 days. It's time to unleash your unique voice to the world!

Let's get started.

1

Day 1. The Messenger Launch Plan

In the blink of an eye, a website can go from nothing to a viral sensation. YouTube first flickered to life in 2005. It could have easily vanished into the dusty corners of failed tech startups. The resolute founders turned early struggles into monumental success. They did this by being optimistic and resilient. They also refused to cut corners.

YouTube's origin story has become legendary. Who hasn't heard about the site where you can watch everything from cute puppies to how-to videos? But before the viral fame and billion-dollar buyout, it was just a sparse website. Only a few visitors trickled in. Uploading video was still complicated for most people, and watching online drained bandwidth.

Despite humble beginnings, the founders persevered. They upgraded the technology, forged partnerships, and enhanced the user experience. Bit by bit, YouTube took shape as not just a video site but a vibrant community. YouTube became a smash sensation overnight. [1]This happened only a year after revamping its strategy.

The creators didn't try boiling the ocean on day one or expect instant results. They laid a thoughtful foundation focused on users' needs. Having the right building blocks in place allows your new online platform to gather steam and thrive.

This chapter reveals the step-by-step game plan to launch your site for successful takeoff, not quick failure. Let's start assembling the launch pad to your success story!

Day 1. The Messenger Launch Plan

Most people launch online platforms haphazardly without much of a plan. This haphazard approach often causes new personal brands and websites to flounder right out of the gate. They launch without a strategy. As a result, they often fail to attract an engaged audience.

Some common mistakes include:

- Failing to differentiate your brand clearly.

- Weak visual branding and messaging.

- Poor website setup that confuses visitors.

- Launching without much content ready.

- Neglecting promotion.

Without differentiation, you blend into the noisy online crowd. Weak branding fails to connect emotionally or project professionalism. A confusing website drives visitors away fast. No content means no reason for people to stick around and engage. And with no promotion, even the best site withers in obscurity.

What's the alternative? A successful launch requires an intentional, structured approach. You need to take the time upfront to lay the proper foundation. This means defining your unique brand voice clearly and dialing into your ideal audience. It involves crafting a visual identity and core messaging that pops.

You need to set up your website to capture prospects immediately. Have core pages and initial content ready to engage visitors. Promoting a compelling brand story gives you initial momentum.

In other words, a structured launch process allows you to systematically build an audience and tribe right from the very start. It kickstarts your efforts onto the path of sustainable success. The good news is the book provides you with a simple launch plan to make all of this happen in 21 days or less. So, let's walk through exactly what that looks like.

Step 1. Develop Your Brand Voice

The first step is developing your brand voice. Your brand voice is essentially the unique way you share your message. It's the style and personality you project through your content and messaging.

Just as every person has their own voice literally, your brand needs its own figurative voice. This voice should ideally align with your natural personality and interests.

There are actually 12 core brand voice archetypes to choose from. Examples include the Sage, the Explorer, and the Hero. Each archetype attracts a different kind of audience. It is crucial to select the right brand voice that fits you authentically. This is important for connecting with your ideal audience from the start.

Let's say, as an example, your brand voice archetype is the Sage. This voice uses wit and wisdom to educate audiences. Use the rugged Explorer voice to attract outdoor adventurers, not intellectuals.

In the next chapter, we'll cover each of the twelve brand voices in more depth. The key takeaway for now is understanding the importance of identifying your natural brand voice. This allows you to start engaging the audience that is a great fit for you right from the beginning. Don't try to be everything for everyone. Dial into the voice made for your tribe.

Step 2. Define Your Brand Strategy

Once you've defined your brand voice, the next step is determining your brand strategy. This includes establishing your visual identity through elements like colors, fonts, and logos. It also includes picking your domain name.

Your visuals are incredibly important because colors and images instantly impact emotions. When people see your brand colors and logo, you want them to feel drawn in by what they say about you.

For example, Coca-Cola's bold red and white colors and flowing script logo build feelings of vitality and Americana. From the beginning, their visual identity strategically attracted thirsty customers.

So, take time to carefully select your color palette, typography, logo design, and domain name. These strategic branding choices build instant recognition and authority. They allow people to form positive associations with you right away. We'll cover this more in chapters three through six.

Step 3. Craft Your Brand Story

You have your brand voice defined. Your visual brand strategy is set. Now, it's time to focus on crafting your core brand story.

Your brand story is the crucial messaging and positioning conveyed through your website. It's especially important on your homepage. This is your first impression - and you only get one chance to get it right.

The copy, positioning, and messaging must instantly resonate with your target audience. It should clearly speak to their hopes, dreams, and struggles. Visitors will quickly click away if your brand story falls flat or feels generic.

For example, research shows that a compelling brand story can improve conversion rates by over 85%. However, weak or unfocused messaging has the opposite effect.

So, take the time upfront to craft your brand story carefully. Let it truly capture the imagination of the audience you want to attract. Make it about them - not you. Speak to their burning needs and desires.

An on-point brand story triggers an instant feeling of "You're speaking directly to me!" in your ideal visitor. This emotional connection is invaluable, so don't gloss over this step. In chapters seven through ten, we will unpack a proven brand story framework for you.

Step 4. Set Up Your Website Pipeline

You've set the stage by defining your brand voice, honing your visual identity, and crafting your core brand story. Now, it's time to set up the core pipeline on your website.

The pipeline involves the follow-up sequence after someone visits your site and signs up or expresses interest. It's the pathway you guide them down from visitor to lead to customer.

Many people mistakenly expect one-and-done sales from a single site visit. But the money is in the follow-up, as the saying goes. An automated and thoughtful pipeline turns interested visitors into engaged subscribers. Ultimately, it turns them into buyers.

For example, someone signs up for your email list. Your follow-up pipeline then delivers a sequence of 5-7 emails over the next week. Each email provides valuable content and moves them along the sales process until they convert.

Don't just expect instant conversions. Take the time to map out this pipeline. Nurture your prospects through an intentional path to becoming customers. This pipeline fuels long-term business growth. In chapters twelve through fifteen, I'll share with you a powerful automated prospect funnel you can easily set up.

Step 5. Build Out Your Core Website Pages

You've got your website homepage set up. But you can't stop there. To fully engage visitors, you need to build out additional core pages on your site. These provide further value and next steps for interested prospects.

Some key pages to focus on include:

- About Page - Tell us about your backstory, passion, and mission. Builds trust.

- Services Page - Details your offerings and their benefits. Fuels sales.

- Contact Page - This makes it easy for visitors to get in touch. Enables leads.

- Blog or Content Page - Share your latest published content. Drives engagement.

- Resources Page - Provides free value upfront, like checklists or downloads. Captures prospects.

Develop these crucial website pages upfront. They inform visitors, inspire them to keep exploring, and prompt them to take action.

For example, Steve Jobs insisted early Apple websites have detailed product pages to draw in and engage visitors fully.

In summary, core website pages help you:

- Build credibility through your backstory.

- Show the value you provide.

- Make it easy for visitors to reach out.

- Give visitors reasons to stick around and consume content.

- Capture leads through free resources and opt-ins.

The key takeaway is not to just focus on your homepage. Build out key pages to inspire engagement from website visitors. We'll unpack this more in chapters sixteen and seventeen.

Step 6. Launch Your Core Blog Content

Your foundation is set with a defined brand voice, a compelling brand story, and a website designed to convert visitors. Now, it's time to start launching content.

Consistently publish fresh content, like blog posts, videos, and podcasts. This gives people reasons to visit your site. It also helps them stick around. It demonstrates your expertise. Content helps attract search traffic. And it fuels your pipeline.

Too many people wait months after launching before they publish any content. That leaves a barren site with little to engage prospects. Don't make that mistake.

Start blogging or publishing videos immediately, even as you build up a consistent content schedule. Loading up initial content populates your site and provides reasons for people to visit your site often.

Regular new content is like a fisherman consistently putting out new bait to attract fish. You draw in your audience with each piece you publish. In chapter eighteen, I'll share my favorite blog post templates.

Step 7. Attract Your First Subscribers

You've built a compelling platform foundation, crafted a conversion-focused website, and published initial content. It's time to promote your new brand and start actively building an audience.

Many people mistakenly think, "if you build it, they will come." But without promotion, even the best website languishes in obscurity. You need to get the word out.

Start promoting your new brand through social media. Also, try guest posting on other sites. Pursue strategic partnerships and any other grassroots channels available.

For example, in Airbnb's early days, they partnered with influential travel bloggers. This helped drive initial interest and pick up traction.

Promoting your platform gives you momentum right out of the gate. Don't keep it a secret - get out there and actively spread the word.

Connect with your first fans. Offer incentives for shares. Attract initial prospects to accelerate growth. We'll lay out all of the steps for you in chapters nineteen through twenty-one.

Day 1 Exercise: Create a Simple Launch Plan Draft

To start putting these launch steps into action, do this quick 10-minute exercise:

Grab a sheet of paper or open a new document. Write down "My Launch Plan" at the top.

Then, under that heading, write the numbers 1 through 7 down the left side. These represent the seven launch steps we covered in this chapter.

Next to each number, jot down just 1-2 words about how you could apply that launch step for your new website or platform.

For example:

1. Brand voice - Friendly teacher

2. Brand strategy - Soothing blue colors

3. Brand story - Help struggling single moms

Spend 5-10 minutes brainstorming your own simple notes for each step. This will get your launch juices flowing!

The point is not to overwhelm yourself by implementing everything right now. Just start mapping out some initial launch ideas.

As you progress through the rest of the book, we'll fully cover how to execute each step. So right now, start visualizing how to apply this strategic launch blueprint to your unique brand.

By taking a few minutes to think through your own plan, you'll build momentum and set the stage for a successful launch!

Day 1 Key Takeaways:

- Follow an intentional, structured plan - don't just wing it.

- Lay the proper brand foundation upfront before creating your website.

- Design your website to convert visitors from the first click.

- Create core content and promote actively right away.

2

Day 2. Define Your Brand Voice

When 27-year-old Estée Lauder started her cosmetics company in 1946, the odds were against her. The industry was dominated by big, masculine brands like Max Factor and Elizabeth Arden. But Lauder envisioned bringing elegance and glamour to the everyday woman.

She crafted a distinctive brand voice aligned with that purpose from the start. Lauder combined European sophistication with American directness. She spoke to women as she would a friend. Her copy and ads conveyed the values of intimacy, beauty, and empowerment.

Competitors stuck to stale, scientific language about "corrective cosmetics." Lauder invited women to reveal their radiance. She promised her products would help you feel glamorous and adored.

Lauder had tapped into the archetype of the Lover - she was selling a feeling, an emotional experience. This cohesive brand voice built fierce loyalty, which fueled meteoric success.

Estée Lauder shows the power of defining your authentic brand voice using archetypes. This chapter will explore the 12 brand voices. You can attract your ideal audience more easily by leaning into your primary brand voice.[2]

Your brand voice is the unique personality you project. It helps you connect with your ideal audience. Your website is not for everyone.

In the words of Meredith Hill, "When you speak to everyone, you speak to no one." [3]

This chapter explains the 12 brand archetypes (also known as brand voices). It also explains selecting the right "voice" to attract your ideal audience. An authentic brand voice sparks emotional bonds with people who share your worldview. Getting this wrong means disjointed messaging that never truly resonates. But align your voice to your values, and you'll magnetically draw your tribe.

Most businesses never intentionally define their brand voice. Their messaging is disjointed across platforms, lacking cohesion. This confusing hodgepodge fails to engage anyone deeply.

Customers can't form emotional bonds with your company without a consistent brand voice. Messaging seems corporate and robotic. However, brand loyalty is built on shared beliefs and values. No one sticks around if your brand seems lifeless.

Don't take a disjointed approach. Instead, strategically craft your brand voice using Jung's 12 archetypes[4]. Identify which "vibe" aligns with your core purpose and audience. Convey your personality consistently across all touchpoints. An authentic brand voice forges emotional bonds with people who share your worldview.

Day 2. Define Your Brand Voice (The 12 Brand Archetypes)

The concept of brand archetypes originated in the work of psychologist Carl Jung. In his book Psychological Types, Jung proposed that human behavior falls into four essential "functions." These are thinking, feeling, intuition, and sensation.

Over the years, theorists have expanded on Jung's four types. They have identified 12 brand archetypes.

These archetypes capture the full range of human motivations and values. Understanding these 12 archetypes helps you strategically craft your brand voice.

The Brand Voice Wheel

I want to introduce you to a helpful tool I call the Brand Voice Wheel. The Brand Voice Wheel has twelve unique brand voices. Your brand voice becomes the basis to connect with your audience.

As you lean into your brand voice, you create an attractive character that has a unique voice, tone, and visual identity for your brand.

Before we dive into the uniqueness of each brand voice, let me point out a few important points.

1. **Knowing your primary brand voice will enable you to attract your ideal audience to your business better.** For example, lean into the Outlaw Brand Voice if you want your business to attract freedom-loving risk-takers. Your brand voice acts like a magnet, drawing in people who resonate with that archetype. Defining this clearly makes it easier for your tribe to recognize your shared values and worldview.

2. **There are four primary quadrants:** The brand voice wheel is divided into the key motivations that drive human behavior - leaving a legacy, connecting with others, serving needs, and seeking truth. Understanding these core drivers helps you narrow down the right brand voice for you.

3. **Inside each of the four quadrants, you have three unique brand voice expressions:** For example, the Leave a Legacy quadrant contains the Outlaw, the Magician, and the Hero brand voices. Each one has subtle differences in personality and messaging while sharing that central ambition.

Now, let's take a closer look at each quadrant and the brand voices under each.

Category 1. The Leave a Legacy Archetypes

Historically, iconic individuals like Marie Curie, Elon Musk, and Rosa Parks have overcome immense obstacles. They have transformed culture, advanced society, and revolutionized industries. They leveraged courage, grit, and vision to blaze new trails and redefine categories. Their accomplishments and contributions forever changed the trajectory of the human race. Brands that tap into the Leave a Legacy archetypes harness this idea. They overcome challenges in daring ways. They make bold impacts. They disrupt the status quo and advance collective ambitions of what's possible.

Brands that use the "leave a legacy" archetypes speak to the trailblazers and innovators in all of us. They motivate us to reach past limiting beliefs and constraints. They help us achieve greatness and meaningful change. Legacy brands capture our aspirations. They help us imagine better realities and manifest them through skill and perseverance. Like pioneers before them, these brands inspire greatness in their customers. They demand it through positioning that calls us to purpose and potential. They reflect the pinnacle of human capability. Let's look closer at the Outlaw, Magician, and Hero brand voices.

The Outlaw

The Outlaw archetype values disruption, rebellion, and bucking the status quo. Brands that tap into this archetype often position themselves as gritty and daring. They are not afraid to break the rules or challenge conventions. They prize independence, risk-taking, and pioneering new territory. Famous Outlaw brands include Harley-Davidson and Axe.

The Magician

The Magician archetype is all about transformation, innovation, and making the impossible possible. This happens through cleverness and vision. Magician brands are inventive trailblazers who surprise and delight their audiences. They tap into people's desires to experience wonder and magic. Well-known brands that embody the Magician archetype include Apple and Cirque du Soleil.

The Hero

Hero brands inspire us to reach our potential and achieve great things. They do this through mastery, courage, and overcoming adversity. They motivate people to strive, compete, and push boundaries. Brands that leverage the Hero archetype include Nike with its "Just Do It" slogan and the U.S. Army with its "Be All You Can Be" positioning. Heroes give us strength, inspire us to action, and make us believe we can be epic.

Category 2. The Pursue Connection Archetypes

Humans have an innate and profound need for belonging, intimacy, and community. Iconic stories from Aristotle to Avatar explore relationships as the cornerstone of meaning and fulfillment. Brands that tap into the Pursue Connection archetypes express our desire for bonds. They tap powerful themes of love, friendship, and camaraderie.

These brands capture our desire for pleasure. They also capture our desire for lighthearted play and the comfort of being seen and embraced as we are. Pursue Connection brands stoke the flames of romance. They fan the spirit of festivity and bring out the best in humanity. Their positions are grounded in togetherness. Their promise calls us toward realizing meaning through vulnerable, authentic relationships. Let's look at the three Pursue Connection Brand Voices.

The Lover

The Lover archetype uses themes of romance, beauty, and sensuality. It forges intimate connections with consumers. Loved brands like Godiva Chocolate and Victoria's Secret play on people's desires, passions, and affections. They use alluring, emotive advertising and positioning. They delight the senses, evoking feelings of being cherished and indulged in life's finer pleasures.

The Jester

The Jester archetype brings out play, celebration, and a lighthearted spirit. Brands like LEGO and Coca-Cola use themes of fun and humor to delight audiences. They position their products as ways to add joy and levity to life. Jester brands emphasize silly, whimsical impressions over serious ones. They seek to amuse and entertain their customers. They deal in laughter, festivity, and childlike wonder.

The Everyman

The Everyman archetype focuses on simplicity, belonging, and working-class appeal. Brands like Home Depot and Dove tap into the Everyman. They position themselves as authentic, approachable, and created to help ordinary people. Their messaging feels homespun and familiar versus glamorous. They deal in community, camaraderie, and celebrating real-world heroes. They honor people who persevere and get the job done.

Category 3. The Provide Service Archetypes

Throughout history, selfless caregivers have made immense positive impacts through service. Brands that leverage the Provide Service archetypes tap into these roles. They speak to our aspiration of belonging to communities that uplift, lead, and create a better world.

These brands meet needs by conveying nurture and care. They also communicate competence and quality or manifest innovations that elevate and delight. Service archetypes promise order and enrichment. They tap our most altruistic motivations and civic virtues. Their messaging calls us to realize a higher purpose. It uses structures and systems that stabilize, lead and progress society. Let's take a closer look at the Caregiver, Ruler, and Creator brand voices.

The Caregiver

The Caregiver archetype meets needs through compassion, generosity, and profound service orientation. Brands like Johnson & Johnson tap into nurturing themes to convey reliability, care, and good stewardship. Their messaging emphasizes community responsibility. It cultivates loyalty through uplifting and empowerment versus self-centered aims.

The Ruler

The Ruler archetype conveys leadership competence, expertise, and hard-won mastery. Ruler brands like Rolex and Mercedes-Benz tap into desires for quality craftsmanship and status. They communicate success themes of achievement, confidence, and elite access. These are earned through determined effort. Their messaging calls us to realize discipline and ambition.

The Creator

The Creator archetype is grounded in invoking imagination, originality, and vision. Brands like Lego and Crayola tap into themes of ingenuity, self-expression, and playful creativity. They deal in fostering exploration and childlike wonder. The creator brand's messaging emphasizes venturing beyond the status quo. The brand showcases breakthrough innovations designed to inspire.

Category 4. The Seek Truth Archetypes

Brands that use the Seek Truth archetypes fulfill our deepest needs for safety, understanding, and freedom. They deal with themes of morality, idealism, wisdom, and adventure. Their stories speak to our noblest aspirations and who we wish to become.

Seek Truth brands promise hope, discovery, and liberation from ignorance. Their messaging calls us to transcend through righteous living, contemplation, and fearless exploration. They convey goodness and hard-won mastery. They also capture ambitions of realizing fuller potential. When we engage these brands, we embark on existential journeys. We seek more authentic versions of ourselves and the world we wish to inhabit. Let's dive into the Innocent, Sage, and Explorer brand types.

The Innocent

The Innocent archetype conveys moral virtue and idyllic impressions. It uses sincerity, goodness, and childlike optimism. Brands like Coca-Cola and Hallmark tap into themes of nostalgia, patriotism, and wholesomeness. They aim to elevate hopes of realizing a more just world where people treat each other well. Their messaging provides comfort through innocence versus exposing harsher realities.

The Sage

The Sage archetype grounds its messaging in disseminating wisdom, intelligence, and truth. Brands like Harvard and TED Talk tap into themes of cutting insight, philosophy, and vision. They aim to stimulate deeper understanding. They unpack mastery and bigger-picture perspectives. They provide enlightening ideas that create elevated outlooks.

The Explorer

The Explorer archetype captures themes of ambition, independence, and venturing into the unknown. Brands like Jeep and National Geographic tap into desires to live wholly on our own terms. They do this through adventure and fearlessly charting new territory. Their messaging calls people to push boundaries. It also urges them to live authentically and realize fuller expressions of freedom.

Aligning your brand voice with one or more of these archetypes helps you connect with your ideal audience on a deeper level. The archetype should resonate with your core values and purpose.

If you would like to take a free online quiz to find your unique brand voice, go to: jmill.biz/brandvoice

Bring Your Brand Voice to Life with AI

So, how do you actually use your brand voice day-to-day? Once you've defined your unique brand voice using the archetypes, you can bring it to life through AI tools. You can create a customized "voice persona" infused with your brand voice instead of outsourcing copywriting.

A voice persona contains key information to help AI write in your distinctive style:

- Personality traits based on your brand archetype

- Examples of your brand messaging

- Key phrases and vocabulary

- An ideal customer profile

- Your brand's mission and values

AI can use this data to generate website copy, blog posts, emails, ads, and other content. It will express your brand voice authentically.

When writing with your voice persona, AI tools will:

- Use personality descriptors matching your archetype

- Incorporate your brand's key phrases and language

- Keep messaging aligned with your values and goals

- Resonate with your ideal customer profile

Refresh your voice persona regularly as your business evolves. However, the ability to outsource copywriting while maintaining your brand voice is a game changer. AI makes it possible to quickly scale communication without losing your unique personality.

Leverage the power of AI writing assistants infused with your archetype-based brand voice. It's invaluable for creating an emotional bond with your ideal audience.

Day 2 Exercise: Select Your Primary Brand Voice

Review the 12 brand voice types earlier in this chapter. List the 2-3 voices that best fit your personality and brand mission.

Next to each voice, write down key messaging phrases or slogans that would align with that voice. Review your list and determine which brand voice feels most authentic to you. Make sure it resonates with your ideal audience. Craft a short brand voice statement that sums up your chosen voice. For example: "My playful, humorous Jester brand voice engages people who don't take life too seriously."

Defining your distinctive brand voice lays the foundation for messaging. This messaging attracts your ideal community. Use this exercise to clarify the perspective you want to project across touchpoints consistently.

If you would like to take a free online quiz to find your unique brand voice, go to: jmill.biz/brandvoice

Day 2 Key Takeaways:

- Strategically choose your brand voice using Jung's 12 archetypes

- Align your voice to your core purpose and target audience

- Express your voice consistently across all touchpoints

- Re-evaluate as your business evolves

- An authentic voice attracts your tribe

3

Day 3. Choose the Right Brand Type

Before Instagram influencers and YouTube celebrities, one man perfected the art of building fame and intrigue around his persona. He was the incomparable P.T. Barnum. Barnum demonstrated the immense power of a personal brand long before the term entered the lexicon. He transformed himself into a cultural spectacle.

In 1853, pre-packaged entertainment was rare. Barnum launched a traveling circus. He called it "P.T. Barnum's Grand Traveling American Museum, Menagerie, Caravan & Hippodrome"[5]. It was a bold, over-the-top extravaganza. The likes of which the public had never experienced. He shamelessly plastered his name across advertisements. He pursued outrageous stunts, sure to whip up controversy. Barnum knew outrage and fascination were two sides of the same coin.

He deliberately cultivated fame and public intrigue. He did this by embodying a flashy, larger-than-life showman persona. Whenever Barnum's name was mentioned, he gave people a compelling reason to pay attention.

Though criticized by some as a relentless self-promoter, no one could argue with his results. Barnum put himself front and center. This forged an emotional, approving bond with the ticket-buying public.

While you don't have to be the center of attention to be successful, this story illustrates the immense power of a personal brand. Directly linking your name with your work can help you break through the noise and capture awareness.

This chapter examines the key differences between personal and private brands. It helps determine the right strategy for your business. Barnum showed that choosing the right brand type may lead to greater profitability and influence.

Day 3. Choose the Right Brand Type

When establishing a new business, one of the most important decisions is building a personal or private brand. Should the founder put themselves center stage as the face of the company? Or keep a degree of separation between their identity and the brand?

Both approaches have upsides and downsides. This section will examine the key differences between personal and private brands. It will help you determine the best strategy based on your goals and aspirations.

Pros of a Personal Brand

A personal brand can help you stand out and connect more deeply with your audience. Consider the example of Brené Brown. She is a research professor who struggled to get traction with her academic work on vulnerability and shame. Things changed when she started talking from her viewpoint and sharing personal stories.

Brown gave a raw TED talk in 2010, opening up about her struggles with vulnerability. The talk exploded, making her a viral sensation. She wrote several #1 New York Times bestsellers, launched a chart-topping podcast, and got her own Netflix special. Her audience feels a powerful connection to her because her work is intensely personal. They see her as a complete human being, not just an expert.[6]

This shows how embracing your personal story and putting yourself front and center can increase your impact. It creates a sense of intimacy and loyalty with your followers. They are drawn to your uncompromising authenticity and willingness to open up. This emotional resonance is hard to replicate with a faceless brand.

Cons of a Personal Brand

While personal branding has many upsides, there are also significant downsides. A personal brand makes you the face of your company, for better or worse. It's like being a celebrity - your reputation is on the line.

Stars like Johnny Depp and Will Smith have faced significant backlash due to personal controversies. Your reputation failures can sink your brand's success. Every mistake and flaw is exposed when your name represents the business. You have minimal privacy or separation between your personal and professional personas.

Also, a personal brand puts immense pressure on you to remain perpetually "on" for your audience. It's like being a politician in the spotlight 24/7. You don't get to have off days or be anything less than perfectly polished. This level of scrutiny can become exhausting over time.

Personal branding is rewarding. However, maintaining your public image requires an incredible amount of work. You'll need thick skin to withstand criticism of both you and your brand. It's important to weigh these challenges before pursuing a personal brand.

Pros of a Private Brand

A private brand allows you to keep the focus on your product or service rather than yourself. This more anonymous approach has its advantages, as the story of Soichiro Honda illustrates.

In 1946, Honda started a company to manufacture motorcycles in post-war Japan. Being an engineer at heart, he named the company after himself but stayed behind the scenes. Honda's brilliance was in product innovation and manufacturing, not self-promotion.

Letting his brand speak through its motorcycles allowed Honda to retain his privacy and personal freedom. The world came to know Honda for its superb engineering and craftsmanship, not the man behind it. This brand separation from the founder allowed the company to evolve beyond one individual.

Honda demonstrates the power of a private brand built on world-class products, not personal hype.[7] It avoids potential perceptions of vanity or ego that can backfire. The focus stays on serving the consumer, not promoting the founder. This subtle, product-centered branding can be exceptionally persuasive.

Cons of a Private Brand

A private brand may seem simpler by avoiding personal publicity. However, this approach has significant drawbacks. A private brand can struggle to connect emotionally with consumers without a face attached. It's like conversing with a blank wall versus a warm, expressive person.

People are drawn to other human beings, not abstract entities. Building affinity and trust in crowded marketplaces is challenging for a faceless company. Why should I care about Brand X when there's no visionary founder's story or transparent values system to make it compelling?

Also, private brands need to have built-in evangelists. People are far more likely to advocate for leaders they feel connected to, like Elon Musk or Oprah, rather than vague corporate brands. Cultivating a devoted user base around a vague, impersonal business is harder.

While avoiding public scrutiny, private brands miss out on the passion and loyalty inspired by putting a human face on a company. This can limit growth and impact over the long term.

Day 3 Exercise: Create a T-Chart to Decide Your Brand Type

Draw a T-chart. On one side, jot down all the benefits you would receive for building a personal brand. Conversely, consider all the benefits of creating a private brand. Whichever side you fill out more indicates the brand path you should go down.

Day 3 Key Takeaways:

- Understanding your goals and comfort level is key to choosing between a personal or private brand.

- Personal brands offer significant benefits like authenticity, flexibility, recognition, human connection, and storytelling.

- Building a personal brand has challenges, such as limited growth, relying on others, planning for the future, and being active online.

- Private brands are great for growing teams, building assets, reducing risk, and looking professional.

- Private brands may face setbacks like a lack of personality, less personal connection, limited flexibility, limited storytelling, and higher initial costs.

4

Day 4. Pick the Right Domain Name

H enry Ford changed history when he founded the Ford Motor Company in 1903. But before selling a single car, he faced a major decision - what to name his new automotive brand.

Many advised Ford to choose a more elaborate name to convey quality and prestige. But he resisted. Ford believed in the power of simplicity. He wanted a name that was short, easy to remember, and would stand out from the competition.

Despite warnings a plain name like "Ford" might be too simple, Henry followed his instincts. He recognized a short, catchy name would easily stick in people's minds. And he was right. The name Ford became instantly recognizable as the company grew to dominate the auto industry.[8]

This fascinating story from history demonstrates the importance of choosing the right name for your brand. Like Ford, opt for a simple, memorable name that communicates your message when picking your domain as an author, coach, or speaker.

Day 4. Pick the Right Domain Name

Many people rush into a decision when picking a domain name without thinking it through. This leads to names that are hard to remember or spell, similar to competitors, or don't represent their brand well. These names also limit the ability to grow a business later on.

Common mistakes include choosing long or complicated names with odd spellings. Another mistake is selecting little-known domain extensions like .info or .site. Many people also neglect to research trademark violations. They also forget to check if matching social media usernames are available.

Instead, thoughtfully come up with and evaluate multiple options. Apply criteria like memorability, uniqueness, brand alignment, and potential for growth. Use online tools to thoroughly check if potential domains and social media usernames are available.

Then, choose the best available option that aligns with your brand and has room to expand. Taking the time upfront to pick your domain carefully will benefit you as you build your online presence.

Step 1: Select a short, simple, and memorable domain name

When picking a domain, choose a name that is short, simple, and easy to remember – like a catchy movie title. Don't overload it with complex words or odd spellings.

The key is to focus on how easily your domain name rolls off the tongue. Say your options out loud to ensure they are straightforward and memorable. This will help build brand awareness by making your unique name easy to recall.

Bottom Line: Keep your domain name short, uncomplicated, and catchy to be easily remembered.

Step 2: Ensure it is brandable and scalable

When Amazon started as an online bookstore in 1994, founder Jeff Bezos chose the name Amazon. He chose it because it sounded exotic and conveyed the large-scale success he envisioned.[9]

This cleverly broad name gave Amazon ample room to grow. Amazon expanded far beyond books into many other e-commerce categories.

As marketing expert David Brier says, "A brand is never about what you're doing today; it's about what you could be doing tomorrow."[10]

Choose a name aligned with your brand identity but versatile enough to scale. Even if you mainly blog now, consider something like Li veYourMessage.com to allow for adding podcasts, videos, and more later on.

The key is picking a domain name that reflects your essence but is flexible enough for future expansion into related topics or platforms. Start thinking big picture.

Step 3: Make it easy to pronounce and spell

IKEA succeeded largely because its short, unique name is simple to say and spell.

A study by domain registrar Namecheap found that easy-to-pronounce domains receive over 30% more website traffic.[11]

Avoid odd spellings with confusing pronunciations. Complex names are easily misspelled and forgotten.

The key is to maximize engagement by choosing a domain name that flows smoothly when spoken aloud. Sound out your options aloud, and stay away from tongue twisters.

Bottom Line: To spread brand awareness, select a name people can instantly pronounce and spell when they hear it.

Step 4: Confirm no Trademark Violations

Just as you couldn't open a store called "Nike Sports Gear" without permission, your domain name also can't use trademarked terms without approval.

For example, a company was sued in 2021 for including the trademarked term "Olympics" in its domain[12]. Don't make this costly mistake.

Research to ensure your preferred name doesn't include trademarks. Even common words like Apple or Amazon are off-limits if trademarked in your field.

The key is thoroughly investigating any existing trademarks or brands to avoid infringement. While changing later can be expensive, it's better than a lawsuit.

Bottom Line: Avoid trademarks, or you may pay a lot later on. Do your homework before settling on a domain.

Step 5: Get Matching Social Media Usernames

As digital marketer Neil Patel notes, "Your name is the heart of your brand identity online." Once you've selected your domain, obtain matching usernames on social media sites. Secure versions of your name on platforms like Twitter, LinkedIn, Instagram, and TikTok.

Consistency builds familiarity. Having an identical name across your domain and social media establishes cohesion for your personal brand. The key takeaway is to claim social media accounts that align with your new domain name. This creates seamless brand recognition as followers see you everywhere online.

Bottom Line: Match your social media handles for a steady brand presence wherever people find you.

Day 4 Exercise: Pick Your Domain Name

Spend 10-15 minutes brainstorming at least 20 possible options for your domain and social media handles. Be creative!

Then, narrow down your list by applying the selection criteria outlined in this chapter. Check availability using tools like Namechk. com.

Choose your top contender that's short, brand-aligned, scalable, easy to say and spell, and passes trademark checks.

Secure your final selection swiftly before someone else snags your first choice. The right domain forms a solid foundation for your online platform.

Day 4 Key Takeaways:

- Choose a name that's simple, memorable, and reflects your essence.

- Ensure your name can grow over time as your business evolves.

- Thoroughly vet options to avoid trademark infringement.

- Match your social media handles for consistency.

- Act quickly to lock in your ideal domain and usernames.

5

Day 5. Select Your Brand Colors

I n the early 2000s, fast food giant Subway struggled to differentiate itself from competitors. The branding consisted of muted greens and yellows blending into the restaurant's interior. A new VP of Marketing suggested embracing vibrant green as the dominant brand color. Though controversial, Subway rolled out a bold green and yellow logo redesign across all locations.

Customers immediately took notice of the eye-catching green exterior and interior decor. The color made Subway stand out from muted brown and red competitors. Sales increased as the energetic green branding attracted health-conscious consumers.

This example demonstrates the power of strategic color selection in shaping brand identity.[13] Color is powerful. Brand color choices shape customer perceptions and guide visual identity. As designer Rebecca Swinson said, "Color creates identity. It's one of the most powerful tools for branding."

In this chapter, we'll explore the psychology of color and best practices for choosing brand colors that attract your ideal audience.

Day 5. Select Your Brand Colors

Color evokes emotion. It's the first thing we notice that makes a lasting impression. Different hues trigger different reactions and associations. Brands leverage this to connect with customers on a subconscious, emotional level.

For example, fast food chains often use red and yellow in logos and marketing. Why? Studies show red stimulates excitement and hunger, while yellow conveys joy and optimism. Now you know why you might crave those McDonald's french fries. B2B tech firms, however, often stick to cooler blues and greys to signal professionalism, security, and stability.

Choose brand colors strategically based on your target audience and desired brand personality. Don't leave it to chance. As entrepreneur Reina Calbay said, "Your brand colors communicate without saying a word. Make sure they're telling the right story."

Finding Your Brand's True Colors

Determining the right colors to represent your brand requires some soul-searching. What qualities capture your brand's essence? What emotions do you hope consumers experience when engaging with your product or service? Once you crystallize your brand identity, consult color psychology guides to find your perfect palette. These guides show the emotional associations of colors. Allow science and strategy—not mere preference—to be your guide.

As an example, BigCommerce has a handy color psychology chart. It maps hues to brands' personality traits.

- Red conveys excitement, intensity, and boldness. Use this attention-grabbing color if energy and drama align with your brand values.

- Orange exudes a friendly and enthusiastic spirit. Does your brand aim to connect with consumers through spirited warmth? Orange gets that message across.

- Yellow inspires optimism, creativity, and mental clarity. Brands can use a yellow rose to encourage consumers to see the world through rose-colored glasses.

- Green signals growth, renewal, health, and peacefulness. Consider this color if your brand offers grounding guidance amid life's chaos.\

- Blue means stability, trust, confidence, and reassurance. Financial companies or traditional institutions often leverage blue tones to telegraph credibility.

- Purple embodies imagination, spirituality, and luxury. Purple builds an aura of exclusivity—perfect for premium or luxury brands.

With color associations mapped to traits, identify the attributes you most want to communicate. Some paired colors look good together, but avoid color combos that give mixed messages.

Study Your Competitors

Before picking your palette, research how top brands in your field use color. See what works well for industry leaders and competitors. Make notes about any color patterns you notice. Does one brand dominate or stand out with their palette? Comparing colors can reveal open spaces or help you avoid copying others.

Jot down the exact shade codes of colors that catch your eye. Sites like BrandColors.net compile brand palettes so you can easily reference real examples. You don't need to start from scratch. Find inspiration from proven color trends in your area, then give it your own spin to stand out.

An interior design firm called Becca Interiors saw most competitors using expected dark greens and browns. They stood out by going lighter with peach and sage green. Smart color research means picking a palette that attracts your crowd but stays unique in a busy market.

Pick a Primary Color

Start by selecting one dominant brand color that serves as the core of your visual identity. This primary color will feature heavily in logos, websites, packaging, and other branding. It's the shade most tied to your brand personality.

For example, Tiffany's robin egg blue or Lego's Firehouse red. These signature hues come to mind instantly when consumers think of those brands.

Ask yourself:

- What color best represents my brand values, mood, and tone?

- Which hue stands out while fitting my niche?

- What color would catch my audience's eye on crowded shelves or web searches?

If you sell eco-friendly goods, maybe vivid green makes sense as a primary color. Tech startups often lean on retro teal or orange as bold primaries. Limiting yourself to one dominant color creates cohesion and makes branding instantly recognizable.

Choose Complimentary Colors

Now, build out a full palette by picking 2 to 4 secondary colors that complement your primary hue. Try Coolors.co, which is a free color palette generator. Input your primary color and pick a palette with suitable shades.

Make sure secondary hues reinforce, not distract from, your primary color. Too many random colors look disjointed.

Emily, the founder of Stationery Co, said: "I struggled juggling five pretty colors I liked. Simplifying to a soft blue primary plus two accent shades gave a consistent, elegant look."

Aim for colors spaced evenly across the color wheel for contrast and visual interest. Don't pick multiple shades too close together. Amazon nails this with the bright blue/orange combo – complementary hues maximizing vibrancy and energy.

Design a Style Guide

Record your final brand color palette in an online or printed style guide document. Include the name plus the exact hex code for each color. This ensures consistency across branding, such as logos, websites, and products.

I used a simple Google Doc when I first created my style guide. Today, I use my Canva Pro account, which stores all my logos and colors for easy access.

Interior designer Sara Hughes struggled with inconsistent colors across projects. She said, "Finally, creating a style guide improved my visual branding instantly."

Test, Get Feedback, Iterate

Don't fall in love with your initial colors. Be willing to test options and make changes. Try showcasing logos or webpage mockups in different colors to target demographics. See which combinations elicit the most positive emotional response. Ask end users, colleagues, industry experts, and business partners for honest feedback.

Tweak hues that feel off-brand or get poor reactions. HomeGoods went through four logo color iterations before finally landing on today's burnt orange. Remember, color selection isn't a one-and-done process. As your brand evolves, you can refine the palette.

Day 5 Exercise: Select Your Brand Colors

Now it's your turn to put color psychology guides to work! Set a timer for 5 to 10 minutes and work through these steps:

1. Close your eyes and imagine the core emotion you want people to feel when they encounter your product, service, or brand. Do you want them to feel energized? Calm? Joyful? Trusting? Get clear on the primary feeling driving your brand identity.

2. Next, go to BrandColors.net and make notes next to 2-3 colors matching that target emotion. Circle the color that feels most aligned with your brand's purpose - this will be your dominant primary hue.

3. Use Coolors.co, an online palette generator tool. Input your chosen primary color. Then, output a 5-color complimentary palette suited for your brand. Tweak the secondary shades if needed to reinforce your primary color.

4. Try creating a simple logo mockup with your chosen colors by going to freelogodesign.org. Make minor adjustments to perfect the combo. Ask a friend or colleague for their gut reaction to the colors.

5. Record your final color palette, including official shade names and color codes, in a basic brand style guide document for future use.

Day 5 Key Takeaways:

- Use color psychology to determine the mood you want to convey.

- Research competitor color palettes to find your niche.

- Pick one primary color that anchors your visual identity.

- Select just 2-4 complementary secondary accent colors.

- Document colors in a style guide for consistency.

- Seek feedback and iterate your palette over time.

6

Day 6. Create Your Brand Logo

Southwest Airlines started out small, struggling to compete against the aviation giants of the time. Their lawyer proposed a radical logo - a vibrant red heart, contrasting sharply with the stark jets of rivals. The heart symbolizes warmth, care, and devotion to customer service. Executives first dismissed it but took a chance on the Maverick logo.

The result proved transformative. The lively heart stood out from the cold, generic competitors. It captured Southwest's friendly, people-first essence. As customers connected emotionally with the logo, profits took off.

Today, Southwest is a top global airline with near-universal brand recognition. The classic red heart logo continues to drive loyalty and affection.[14]

This story shows a logo's power to shape identity. Your logo provides the first visual impression of your business.

As expert Guy Kawasaki put it, "A brand is a contract with the consumer. A logo is the visual handshake."

In this chapter, we'll explore DIY and outsourcing options to design a memorable, effective logo reflecting your brand.

Day 6. Create Your Brand Logo

Let's explore three different ways you can get your brand logo designed quickly.

Option 1. DIY Logo Design

Creating your own logo can be quick, easy, and free using online design tools. While the end result may not look as polished as hiring a pro, DIY logos work for simple branding needs.

The biggest advantage of DIY logo design is full creative control. You can play around with shapes, colors, fonts, and concepts until you land on something you love. It also saves a ton of money compared to hiring a designer.

According to Statista, hiring a professional graphic designer costs $200-500 per project. DIY tools are mostly free or offer paid upgrades.

Canva's simple drag-and-drop editor has over 60,000 free templates. They're for logos, social media posts, presentations, and more.

I used Canva to whip up my Thrifty Reseller Hub logo quickly. Thanks to their huge template library, I found something close to my vision and customized it in minutes.

Another popular free tool is FreeLogoDesign.org. It generates customized logo ideas after you input your business name. While the AI suggestions weren't perfect, they sparked new directions I wouldn't have considered.

Lisa, the owner of ReNew Upcycled Furniture, liked how Free Logo Design gave her control over the creative process. "I loved playing around with different fonts, colors, and icons." I probably went through 100 options before finding one that really represented my brand."

The biggest drawback of DIY designs is the finished product can look amateurish. You also need basic graphic design skills.

But for simple logos, DIY provides a quick and cheap way to handle branding yourself.

Option 2. Outsourcing Logo Design

Consider outsourcing logo design to a freelance graphic designer for more professional results.

Hiring an experienced designer saves time and takes the work off your plate. It also yields a higher-quality, visually appealing logo.

Look for freelancers on sites like Fiverr and 99Designs. Prices start around $300.

Fiverr features independent contractors offering logo design services starting at $5 packages. Browse designers by review ratings and sample work until you find someone matching your style and budget needs.

99Designs takes a different approach. You describe your project requirements, and then dozens of designers submit logo options to choose from. This logo design contest format lets you leverage the skills of many creatives.

In a 2021 survey, 99Designs found that 97% of small business owners were satisfied with the logos they received. The broad range of options makes it easy to find a design you love.

For my 50s retro blogging logo, I paid 99Designs $250 to produce over 75 logo variations. Seeing so many creative directions inspired me to pick an unexpected abstract logo I'd never thought of.

Outsourcing can get pricey, but you end up with a high-quality logo customized exactly for your brand. Just make sure to communicate your preferences so designers nail your vision clearly.

Option 3. Hybrid Logo Design

The hybrid route combines DIY and outsourcing. For example, after brainstorming concepts and playing around with DIY tools, you could hire a designer. The designer can refine your rough idea into a polished logo.

Or you can ask a designer to provide 2-3 initial concepts, then use DIY tools to tweak the details of your favorite option.

This gives you more control over the process compared to total outsourcing. It also costs less than fully handing over the reins to a designer.

Jeremy, founder of Vinyl Records Co, used this hybrid approach: "I created a draft logo concept myself using an online logo maker. The designer then took my basic idea and turned it into a sleek, professional design."

Many DIY tools offer add-on services for custom design work. For example, hiring Canva's in-house designers starts at $20 per logo revision.

You can find freelancers to refine and finalize your design concepts on Fiverr for cheap as well.

Just be sure to communicate clearly so designers know which specific elements you want to change or polish. Provide examples of aesthetics and styles you like.

The hybrid route gives you the benefits of DIY creativity plus access to a designer's skills for finishing touches. Just prepare yourself to pay more than if you were doing it yourself.

Evaluating Logo Design Options

How do you select the winner once you have logo options from any creation method? Focus on three criteria:

1. Visual Appeal - Does it look professionally designed and pleasing to the eye?

2. Brand Values - Does it convey your brand identity and resonate with your target audience?

3. Flexibility - Does it work across different formats like websites, business cards, and packaging?

Run your top choices by close friends, colleagues, or trusted early customers. See which they respond to most positively.

Doing so helped Ryan, founder of Open Road Bicycles, realize the logo he loved didn't vibe with customers. He chose a different option that better reflected his brand values after gathering outside feedback.

Don't stress too much about deciding. As your business evolves, you can always update the logos. Focus on finding an appealing, flexible logo that communicates your core brand identity.

The most important thing is taking that first step to define your brand visually with a professional logo!

Day 6 Exercise: Create Four Draft Logos

Select one of the logo tools mentioned earlier (Canva, FreeLogoDesign.org, Fiverr.com, or 99Designs).

Create four logo ideas using your brand colors and representative symbols/imagery.

Snap photos of your rough draft logos and post them on Facebook, Twitter, LinkedIn, or Instagram. Ask friends and connections:

- Which logo is most eye-catching or memorable?

- Which best represents your brand personality and values?

- Would you proudly wear a t-shirt with any of the logos? Which one(s)?

Monitor responses over 24 hours. Tally up votes/reactions for each logo. Combine this social feedback with your own intuitive preferences.

At the end of the exercise, you should have a data-backed top choice or two to develop further. Refine the winner digitally in Canva or hire a designer to finalize your crowd-vetted logo concept.

Testing DIY logo mockups with social crowdsourcing will reveal which embodies your brand essence. It will also show which attracts your audience visually.

Use this quick exercise to craft an effective logo rooted in target market feedback.

Day 6 Key Takeaways:

- DIY tools like Canva provide a quick, cheap route for simple logos.

- Hiring professional designers via Fiverr or 99Designs yields higher quality and custom designs.

- Using a hybrid approach allows you to start a concept and then have a pro refine it.

- Evaluate logo options on visual appeal, brand values, and adaptability.

- Get outside feedback to help select the logo that best represents your brand.

7

Day 7. Your Aspirational Headline

De Beers faced a crisis as a young company - a massive surplus of diamonds but little consumer demand. At the time, most Americans saw diamonds as a luxury only the ultra-wealthy could afford. De Beers hired an ad agency to shift that narrative dramatically.

Rather than focus on the diamonds themselves, they targeted people's deeper emotional desire for romance. This birthed the aspirational 1937 slogan, "A Diamond is Forever." By linking diamonds with everlasting love and commitment, the campaign resonated widely. Over the next decade, U.S. diamond sales exploded by 55% as suitors bought into the idealized promise.[15]

This story reveals the immense power of an aspirational headline. It can shift emotions and capture imaginations. The right words can rapidly transform even seemingly stable industries. They tap into the audience's innermost desires and promise to fulfill long-held dreams.

In this chapter, we'll break down the key steps you need to take to write such a compelling, aspirational headline. Just as "A Diamond is Forever" sparked growth for De Beers, the right headline can set your business apart and fuel its success.

We will be using a proven story-based framework created by Donald Miller from StoryBrand. I'll also be sharing a few tweaks along the way to optimize this for personal brands. Let's get started!

Day 7. Aspirational Headline

To create a headline that converts visitors into leads, focus on crafting an aspirational headline. Aspirational headlines speak to the end goals and dreams of your ideal prospects. They understand what your audience really wants to achieve or become by using your product or service. Some examples:

- Become a travel pro with our training

- Turn your passion into a business

- Join the ranks of elite runners

- Find your dream home here

These headlines promise to help people achieve an aspirational identity or outcome. Let's examine the key steps for writing your own aspirational headline:

1. Define Your Ideal Prospect First

Getting crystal clear on who your ideal customer is should be the very first step in crafting your headline. As legendary sales trainer Zig Ziglar said, "You can't hit a target that you don't have." Before you can create a headline that speaks to your audience's deepest desires, you need to understand who that audience is fully.

Imagine you run a gym and want to attract more members. If you don't define your target market first, your headline could end up appealing to no one. Generic claims like "Get Fit Here" or "Best Gym in Town" don't speak to any specific motivation.

Instead, define your ideal member persona first. For example, let's say you conclude your best prospective members are busy moms in their 30s and 40s who want to lose baby weight and get back in shape. Now, you can craft a more targeted aspirational headline like "Bounce Back After Baby at [Gym Name]." This taps directly into their transformation goal.

The more detailed you can get on your ideal prospects' goals, passions, and struggles, the better. As legendary copywriter David Ogilvy said, "The more you know about your audience, the more likely you are to create advertising that is effective." Do the work upfront to understand your ideal customers. That understanding will pay off. It will help when you write an aspirational headline tailored to them.

2. Understand Their Motivations

Once you have a clear picture of your ideal prospect, the next step is getting inside their head. What deep-down motivations drive their behavior? What outcomes are they really seeking? What problems do they desperately want someone to solve?

This takes empathy and an investigative mindset. An e-commerce company that only focuses on low prices might miss that their customers also care about fast shipping. Dig deeper to discover their core motivations for using online services.

Getting into this investigative mindset is like being a detective at a crime scene, looking for clues. You need to gather all the available data on what makes your ideal prospect tick. Useful sources include customer surveys, focus groups, and social media monitoring. Talking directly to existing customers is also helpful.

As innovation guru Stephen Shapiro explains, "Customers don't always know what they want. Get out of the office and watch people use your products in real-world settings." Go where your ideal prospects are and observe firsthand what frustrations they face and what goals they pursue. This real-world observation can uncover powerful motivations you can leverage in your headline.

If you don't have an audience yet, ask about their goals, passions, and struggles on social media. You can do this on your personal profile or in one of many targeted Facebook groups.

Gather more clues on what your prospects truly care about. Then, you can craft a headline that taps into those core motivations and promises to fulfill their deepest desires. Do your detective work upfront, and you will create a headline that instantly connects with your ideal customers.

3. Focus On Their Transformation

Once you understand your target audience's motivations, you can zero in on the transformation they are seeking. This is how you shift the focus from features to benefits in your headline.

Think of a software company that helps law firms manage their client records. They could tout features like "cloud-based storage" or "automated workflows." But those won't stick in the minds of attorneys seeking to become more organized and efficient.

Instead, focus the headline on their desired transformation. Use "Regain Control of Your Firm With Our Client Management System." This paints a before-and-after story of the change your product enables.

To highlight the transformation, get descriptive. For a personal trainer, that may mean promising to "Take You From Flab to Fit." A cleaning service could say "We Turn Messy Homes Into Spotless Havens."

These headlines create a vivid contrast between where prospects are now versus where your business promises to take them. As copywriting legend John Caples advised, "Paint a vivid word picture of the situation as it will be when your offer has fulfilled its promise."

This imagery is what makes aspirational headlines so compelling. They give prospects a glimpse of the future your business offers. Keep this transformational focus front and center when crafting your headline.

4. Promise Value

Your aspirational headline also needs to make a promise to your prospects. It's not enough to simply describe their hopes and dreams - you need to position your business as the guide they need to achieve their goals.

Consider the iconic Milk Processor Education Program's "Got Milk?" campaign that ran from 1993 to 2014. While catchy, their initial headline didn't communicate concrete value. It was aspirational but vague.

So in 1995, they introduced the tagline "Milk - It Does A Body Good."[16] This promised a clear benefit - drinking milk improves your health. It gave people a compelling reason to buy milk that aligned with their goals.

This promise of value cemented milk's place in the cultural consciousness. The campaign helped boost milk sales by over 20% in just the first year.

Your headline needs to make a similarly direct promise that your business can deliver real value to prospects. Whether that's saving them time, improving their health, or achieving a dream, boil down the core benefits you provide. This concrete value is what convinces visitors to explore further.

5. Be Concise

Now that you've brainstormed ideas and chosen a compelling aspirational headline, the final step is to make it shorter.

Long, wordy headlines fail to make an impact. Consider the Amsterdam Chamber of Commerce's lengthy 1914 slogan:

"Amsterdam, from a navigational perspective the most important city of the Netherlands, located at the intersection of the North Sea Canal and the Amstel river."

While descriptive, only the most patient visitors would make it to the end.

In 1936 they revamped it to the simple phrase: "Amsterdam Has It." This boiled down Amsterdam's essence into three concise, memorable words.

Follow their lead and tighten your headline substantially. Challenge yourself to convey the core essence in 10 words or less. This requires brutal editing. Eliminate any fluff or unnecessary words.

As renowned advertiser David Ogilvy said, "Make it simple. Make it memorable. Make it inviting to look at. Make it fun to read."

Strive for simplicity and brevity in your headline. Tight writing requires hard work, but the effort pays off. A concise, focused headline has far more impact. So keep polishing and trimming until your headline pops.

Common Mistakes

Here are some common mistakes to avoid when crafting your aspirational headline:

- Using industry jargon - Speak plain language your prospects understand.

- Being too generic - Focus on their specific needs and goals vs. generic claims.

- Making it all about you - Keep the focus on their transformation.

- Being boring - Inject emotion, excitement, and benefit into your headline.

- Promising too much - Make claims you can realistically deliver on.

Day 7 Exercise: Brainstorm 20 Aspirational Headlines

Set a timer for 10 minutes and brainstorm at least 20 aspirational headlines for your homepage.

Let the ideas flow without self-editing at first. Make sure they focus on your prospect's transformation. Promise tangible value. Tap into their goals and motivations. If you are struggling, use an AI tool like ChatGPT. Give the tool as much info as you can use the points mentioned earlier and ask it to produce twenty aspirational headlines for you.

Circle the top 3-5 headlines, then narrow down to your favorite. Test it on your homepage and track how it impacts conversions.

Continue to refine until you have a headline that truly resonates with your audience and compels them to take action.

Day 7 Key Takeaways:

- Know your ideal prospect deeply

- Focus on their desires and goals

- Promise to fulfill their aspirations

- Keep it concise and benefit-driven

- Speak directly to your audience

- Revise and refine for maximum impact

8

Day 8. The Big Three

During the Great Depression in the 1930s, many Americans were struggling to afford food for their families. Unemployment was rampant, reaching 25% at its peak. Families stood in soup lines just to get a meager meal. In the midst of this hardship, one voice powerfully connected with the emotional reality people faced. Franklin D. Roosevelt regularly addressed citizens in his "Fireside Chats" over the radio, opening with:

"My friends, I want to talk for a few minutes with the people of the United States about banking..."

He didn't promote his political agenda first. He didn't boast of his expertise and accomplishments as president. He bonded with them as "my friends" who faced difficult times, showing he profoundly understood their struggles. Roosevelt established many critical programs.

For example, he created Social Security, which addressed people's needs and improved lives dramatically. His ability to connect empathetically was a key to his success.[17]

This story demonstrates why truly relating to your audience's frustrations first fosters trust. It also fosters belief in your ability to help them. FDR did just that. Before presenting your solutions, lead with your audience's "Big Three Struggles." The rest will follow.

Day 8. The Big Three

Most websites dump all their services, products, and features on the homepage without an overarching strategy. They use industry jargon that visitors may not understand. The focus is entirely on what the business offers rather than what the visitor needs.

Often, businesses will try to cram everything onto the homepage. There's no greater purpose or flow, just a splattering of products, services, blog posts, testimonials, and more. It's a shotgun approach that hopes something will stick.

Of course, the business knows what each item on the page means. But from an outsider's perspective, it quickly becomes an overwhelming flood of information. The lack of organization makes it tough to find relevance as a visitor.

Businesses also tend to rely heavily on industry terminology. They use the shorthand familiar to insiders without explaining concepts clearly. This leaves visitors confused as terms fly over their heads. Too often, businesses only think about themselves. The homepage becomes a showcase of everything they do and offer. But the visitor doesn't care about the business, at least not yet. They first wonder, "What's in it for me?" The homepage doesn't answer that critical question.

The shotgun approach overwhelms visitors rather than engaging them. Throwing everything out there makes it hard for visitors to connect the dots between their needs and what the business provides. It buries the most relevant connections under an avalanche of information.

Industry jargon flies over most visitors' heads. People understand the world through their own experiences. They don't know the insider terminology without some translation. Leading with language only an expert would understand drives visitors away.

Focusing solely on the business instead of the visitor is a fatal mistake. Homepage visitors ask themselves one question: "How can you help me?" A homepage that only talks about the business fails this basic test. The visitor leaves without having their needs addressed.

A common mistake is trying to cover every service, product, and feature right up front. But different visitors care about different things. Trying to be all things to all people makes it hard for visitors to self-select what fits them. Many businesses use language only insiders would understand. But simple, everyday language is more engaging and accessible to homepage visitors. Avoid industry jargon without context and explanation.

It's easy to fall into the trap of an organization-centric homepage. But focusing on visitors, their pain points, and how you can help is crucial. Don't just talk about yourself - talk about them!

Step 1. Identify the 3 Big Challenges

Start by identifying your audience's top three challenges. What frustrations keep them up at night? What problems and pain points can you relate to and empathize with? As Theodore Levitt famously said, "People don't buy drills. They buy holes." Likewise, people aren't looking for your specific offering at first. They want solutions to their struggles.

Identify what challenges your audience needs to overcome. Reflect these core frustrations and pains back to them upfront. Show you truly get what they're going through.

For example, an organizational consultant could reflect frustrations like:

- Feeling overwhelmed by clutter at home?

- Unable to stay focused and productive at work?

- Stuck in constant reaction mode without progress on goals?

A personal trainer could reflect frustrations like:

- Feeling stuck in an exercise rut?

- Getting easily discouraged and giving up?

- Not seeing results fast enough?

A reflection of "yep, that's me" builds rapport quickly. When visitors see their own emotions and challenges mirrored back, it communicates that you understand their world. Identify the top three pain points your audience faces. This shows you empathize with their situation and builds trust. It makes them receptive to the solutions you'll offer next.

Step 2. Offer 3 Big Solutions

Once you've connected with their frustrations, offer hope by presenting solutions. Identify the three main ways you can provide answers to their pain points. Position yourself as a guide who can clearly simplify the path ahead.

Think of it like a map that highlights only a few fastest routes to get somewhere, cutting through the clutter of side streets and back alleys. You are promising to map out the best and most direct solutions.

For example, that organizational consultant could now promise:

- A proven system to declutter and find focus

- Research-backed tools to be proactive and achieve goals

- Accountability and support to stop reacting and start making progress

That personal trainer could now promise:

- A customized workout program to break through plateaus

- Encouragement and motivation not to quit but to keep improving

- A visible step-by-step plan to stay on track and get results

The key solutions show you don't just empathize but also have concrete ways to help them move forward. Visitors can quickly see how you specifically can guide them to a better place. Offer the three main solutions that can help lead your audience out of their pains and frustrations. Position yourself as the expert guide, ready to simplify and illuminate the path ahead.

Step 3. Add the Challenges and Solutions to the Homepage

With the top 3 frustrations and solutions identified, it's time to lead your homepage with this crucial information. Place the pains and solutions front and center before diving into details.

Consider how a writing coach's homepage might speak to the frustrations and solutions of their audience:

"Overwhelmed by writer's block and self-doubt? Struggling to finish your book? Get the motivation and guidance you need. Our writing courses provide an encouraging community and expert instruction. Learn practical tips to overcome blocks and keep writing. Finish your manuscript with confidence and joy."

This immediately positions the writing coach as empathetic to an author's frustrations and as the solver of those pains. Now, visitors will scroll happily to learn more specifics.

Next, you want to display your three big success steps. If you had to boil down your process to just three things, what would they be? When I did this exercise, I came up with the following:

1. Discover Your Message

2. Launch Your Platform

3. Market Your Message

Each of those three big points contains a lot to unpack, but it provides a simple roadmap that my audience can understand and remember.

Hook homepage visitors by leading with the top 3 pain points they face, along with your three main solutions. Make them feel heard and understood. Provide hope you can guide them forward.

Step 4. Use Clear, Familiar Language

Avoid using industry jargon and specialized terminology only insiders would understand. While impressive to fellow experts, this lingo is over the heads of most homepage visitors.

A study found that industry insiders greatly overestimate how much outsiders comprehend their field's vocabulary. Without explanation, visitors feel overwhelmed and alienated by foreign terms.

Instead, explain topics simply using everyday language familiar to the average person. For example:

- Instead of "leverage agile frameworks," say "learn a flexible approach."

- Instead of "omnichannel synergies," say "consistent experience across the internet."

- Instead of "frictionless human-centered design," say "intuitive, easy-to-use product."

Everyday language welcomes visitors in. Jargon and buzzwords distance them. Speak plainly like you're explaining concepts to a friend, not impressing colleagues.

Avoid insider jargon and specialized terminology without a clear explanation. Converse with visitors using simple, familiar everyday language to engage them more fully.

Step 5. Write in the Second Person

Make your homepage copy feel personalized by addressing the visitor directly using "you" and "your." This conversational tone feels like you're speaking to them versus simply presenting information.

As Einstein observed, "If you can't explain it simply, you don't understand it well enough." Use second-person language to distill complex topics into tidbits that speak directly to each visitor. For example:

- Have you wanted to try meditation but weren't sure where to start?

- Get personalized meditations tailored exactly to your goals.

- You'll get a meditation coach to support your practice every step of the way.

People perk up when information seems tailored specifically for them. Use "you" frequently within the homepage copy. Guide visitors personally rather than broadly discussing concepts.

Day 8 Exercise: Create the Big 3 Challenges & Success Steps

To immediately apply these concepts to your homepage, do this quick 10-minute exercise:

Set a timer for 10 minutes. Grab a blank sheet of paper and a pen. At the top, write "Audience Frustrations." Underneath, brainstorm and jot down the top 5-7 core challenges and pain points your audience faces. Really get into their shoes. If you don't know, ask on social media.

Now under that, write "My Solutions." Jot down the 3-5 main ways you address those visitor challenges. How will you simplify the path ahead?

Finally, open up your homepage. How can you quickly add in three core frustrations and then three solutions using everyday language?

When done, read it aloud. Does it sound like you're speaking directly to someone using simple language? Or is it organization-focused and full of industry lingo?

This quick exercise will help you refine your homepage. It will better attract and engage visitors by leading with empathy and solutions. Set aside 10 minutes to try it out!

Day 8 Key Takeaways:

- Reflect your audience's top frustrations high up on your homepage to show empathy.

- List your three main solutions right after to position yourself as the answer.

- Lead with pains & solutions first before details to set the stage.

- Explain topics simply without jargon using language visitors relate to.

- Use "you" and "your" to speak directly to them about their needs.

9

Day 9. Your Main Call to Action

The year was 2007. Nintendo wanted to launch its groundbreaking Wii gaming console. However, it needed a campaign to show Wii's innovative motion controls. So they created a brilliantly simple call to action: "Wii would like to play." The message was direct, humanizing, and action-oriented. People instantly grasped how the Wii worked and wanted to try it themselves. Sales exploded, and the Wii became a worldwide cultural phenomenon.[18]

Over a century before, circus pioneer P.T. Barnum lured crowds with irresistible calls to action like "This Way to the Egress!" (exit). Once inside, visitors were wowed by his spectacles and unwilling to leave. Through bold commands, Barnum turned tickets into profits.

Like these showmen, you need to speak directly to visitors the moment they enter your website. A clear, customer-focused call to action is crucial for turning awareness into action. This chapter will explore why an unambiguous call to action dramatically boosts conversions. It will also explain how to craft one that compels. Let's learn from creative marketers how distinct directives engage and convert.

Day 9. Your Main Call to Action

Your website homepage is like the front door to your business. It's the first impression visitors get of who you are and what you offer.

Most homepages, unfortunately, fail to make a strong impression. They lack clarity on what the business does and what action the visitor should take next. It's as vague and uninviting as a front door with no knocker or doorbell.

This chapter will explain why you need to display a main call to action on your homepage. We'll explore common mistakes people make in this area and how to create a compelling call to action that converts visitors into leads. You'll learn a step-by-step framework for crafting the right messaging and visuals. This will prompt your ideal customer to take their crucial first step with you.

An effective call to action is one of the most important elements for launching your platform online. With a clear and prominent call to action, you can turn your website from a digital brochure into a lead-generating machine. Let's get started on creating one that works.

Most homepages lack a singular, unambiguous call to action. Instead, they have generic text like "Learn More" or "Contact Us" as their primary button. Or they rely solely on their navigation menu for visitors to choose their own path. The problem? This provides no clear direction on what you want users to do first. Without specifics on the intended action, visitors feel disoriented. Studies show that giving users too many options reduces conversions by as much as 40%.

A vague call to action fails for three reasons:

1. It requires too much thinking. Visitors want to know right away what you want them to do. Forcing them to stop and evaluate options creates friction.

2. It kills urgency. Strong calls to action use action verbs that

convey the need to act now, like "Start Today" or "Get Your Free Guide." Non-specific calls to action communicate no urgency.

3. It doesn't speak to customer intent. Visitors come to your site with a specific intent—to solve a problem, get answers, or satisfy a need. A generic call to action does not address their motivation.

An effective call to action directly responds to what brought the visitor to your site. It gives them an obvious next step that moves them closer to fulfilling their intent. Here's a step-by-step framework for creating one that converts:

1. Identify Your Visitor's Intent

Put yourself in your target customer's shoes. What need or desire brought them to your site? What problem do they want solved? Your call to action should promise to address their intent.

Let's say you run an online cookware store. Visitors arrive at your site looking for help cooking faster, healthier meals. Your call to action should speak directly to that intent. Something like "Get my 5-day meal prep guide" or "Download 100+ quick & easy recipes."

To identify intent, engage in an exercise corporate strategists call the Five Whys. Keep asking why visitors come to your site until you get to the root.

Why do they come to my site?

- To find new cookware - But why do they want new cookware?

- To cook meals faster - Why do they want to cook faster?

- To eat healthier - Why is that important?

- To lose weight and have more energy.

Boom! That's the intent your call to action should address. As organizational guru Simon Sinek says, "People don't buy what you do, they buy why you do it." Structure your call to action around their deeper why.

2. Lead With Action Verbs

Use commanding action verbs that convey urgency, like "Start," "Join," or "Download." Avoid passive verbs like "Learn more." Action verbs get attention and create momentum. They imply that the desired action will lead to a positive end result.

For example, "Download our home buying checklist" sounds more compelling than "Learn about our home buying process."

"Download" implies receiving a concrete tool to aid in home ownership. "Learn" sounds vague and nonspecific. Strive to use simple, one-syllable action verbs. Here are some great options for calls to action: Get, Try, Buy, Join, Start, Order, Reserve, Download, Watch, Listen, Read, and Begin.

Ask yourself if each word packs a punch. Does it spark immediate interest and a sense of urgency? The right action verb will get visitors itching to click your call to action button.

3. Speak to Their Self-Interest

Promote the benefits they'll receive by taking action, not features. For example, say "Download Your Stress Management Toolkit" vs. "Download a PDF."

Effective calls to action appeal to the visitor's self-interest - how they will personally benefit. Highlight the concrete outcome of following your call, not just the action itself.

President Franklin D. Roosevelt applied this tactic in his campaign for the New Deal programs. He didn't use bureaucratic language about policy changes. Instead, he focused his messaging on how Americans would benefit. His famous refrain, "a chicken in every pot and a car in every garage," painted a vivid picture of prosperity for all.

Like FDR, boil down what's in it for the customer. For a financial advisor, instead of "Download my investing guide," try "Secure your retirement dreams." By speaking directly to their concerns, you spark action.

4. Be Specific

Tell them exactly what form the action takes. Is it to download a guide, watch a video, or sign up for a free trial?

Vague calls to action are like a store clerk who says, "Let me know if you need anything," versus one who asks, "Would you like to try that on?" Specificity removes doubt.

When Chipotle trained staff to ask, "Would you like chips or a drink with that?" rather than "Anything else?" sales of soda and sides increased.

Like the Chipotle staff, explicitly state what you want visitors to do. Say "Download My 7-Day Meal Plan" instead of "Get Cooking!"

Use clear nouns like "guide," "checklist," or "class." Quantify with timeframes like "30-minute video masterclass."

With increased specificity, you'll likely see increased conversion rates just like Chipotle did. Remove ambiguity and watch more visitors take your desired action.

Common Mistakes

The two most common mistakes are using a vague call to action or having no singularly obvious call to action. Other pitfalls include:

- Burying it below the fold so visitors have to scroll to find it

- Making it visually blend in instead of stand out

- Using confusing language like industry jargon or unfamiliar terms

- Asking for too much upfront, like phone number and mailing address

An optimized call to action allows you to guide visitors seamlessly into becoming leads.

Day 9 Exercise: Decide Your Main Call to Action

To create a compelling call to action, follow these three steps:

1. Study any calls to action on competitor or non-competitor websites you admire. What works about their messaging, design, and placement?

2. Draft 5 different phrasings for your call to action based on this chapter's guidelines.

3. Test the different versions on your site and track conversion rates. This can be done manually or using affordable A/B

testing software.

With a great call to action, you have a 24/7 salesperson on your site, prompting visitors to convert.

Day 9 Key Takeaways:

- Speak directly to your visitor's intent with a customer-focused promise

- Lead with action verbs that convey urgency

- Be specific on the action requested and link directly to the next step

10

Day 10. Craft Your Brand Story Home Page

Donald Miller never set out to build a marketing empire. The Christian memoir writer is known for vulnerably-crafted books. He cultivated a small but fervent fanbase. Yet, as his blog and speaking engagements gained traction, Miller felt something was still missing.

Audience engagement remained surface-level. His core concepts failed to resonate fully after the seminars ended. Miller hadn't translated his ideas into practical application in the real world.

This sparked Miller's epiphany. He began studying how big brands like Nike and Apple clearly communicate value. They do this by tapping into stories etched deep in the consumer psyche. Miller realized he could help companies speak directly to their customers' deeper motivations. He would do this by focusing less on features and more on aspirations.

Drawing lessons from classics like The Hero's Journey, Miller developed his StoryBrand Framework around 2013.[19] It's a proven seven-part storytelling method now used by over 500,000 brands globally.

The StoryBrand process breaks through noise and connects consumers at an emotional level. It calls the customer the hero on a transformative quest. The brand serves as their guide, providing a clear path forward when failure seems imminent. Ultimate success is a narrow possibility worth fighting for. The StoryBrand framework is divided into seven parts:

1. Hero - references the customer as the hero of the story

2. Problem - focuses on the customer's problem

3. Guide - introduces your brand as the guide

4. Plan - provides the step-by-step plan for success

5. Call to Action - asks the customer to take action

6. Success - paints a picture of the success customers enjoy

7. Failure - warns what failure looks like if no action is taken

So far in our journey, we've covered the core elements every strong homepage needs. These include:

- An aspirational headline that speaks to ideal visitors' deepest hopes

- Listing the top three challenges holding them back from realizing their goals

- Your three-step formula to guide them to success

- And lastly, a prominent call-to-action button to get them started toward their dreams.

In this chapter, we build on that foundation. We'll illustrate how to weave those critical pieces into an inspirational Brand Story homepage. This homepage makes visitors the heroes. We'll craft a high-impact homepage that persuades readers to join our cause by combining compelling copy, strategic design, and putting the visitor experience front and center. No code or tech skills are required.

You're now ready to guide visitors confidently through the customer journey you envision for them with this bold Brand Story blueprint. We're moving from theory to application - let's put these concepts into practice with clear examples.

Day 10. Create Your Brand Story Home Page

Most personal brands lead their homepages by touting themselves as the hero. They splash logos and headshots front and center. This self-focused approach fails to resonate emotionally or convey core values to visitors.

Effective homepages make the ideal audience the hero of the story instead. They speak directly to visitors' aspirations and pain points with targeted messaging. For example, "You want to write a book but don't know where to start..." demonstrates empathy and establishes common ground.

Savvy personal brands guide visitors down a path by making them the central character. A homepage headline like "Write Your Way Onto the Bestseller List" encourages readers to imagine achieving their wildest dreams.

Empathetic copy provides a wise guide for confused visitors. They want to transform their manuscripts into published masterpieces but may not know the next steps.

The key is crafting a visitor-focused narrative. Make ideal visitors the inspirational central characters and position your brand as their guide. Meet visitors where they are in their journey before asking them to take action. Esteemed teachers throughout history have used this servant leadership approach to lasting influence.

Step 1. Use a Template

When mapping out your homepage, resist the urge to start building it in your website builder immediately. That's like an architect diving into construction blueprints before conceptually planning the building's purpose and layout.

I've created a drag-and-drop homepage wireframe template using Canva. Wireframing allows you to strategically map out the critical elements your homepage needs. It also shows how visitors will flow through it. The good news is you don't need to be a graphic designer to use this tool. Just go to JMill.biz/wireframe to get free access to my Canva template.

The Canva templates have placeholders for you to map the customer's journey visually. You can experiment with what messaging works best by dropping in sample headlines, captions, images, and buttons before going live. Think of it like an artist's sketch before painting the full mural.

Approaching your homepage as a storyboarding process keeps the focus on customer experience rather than just features. The goal is to craft a compelling homepage brand story. This story should make visitors the heroes and present your business as their helpful guide. This sets the stage for an aligned journey across every subsequent page.

Step 2. Add Your Content to the Wireframe Template

Now that you have access to the homepage wireframe in Canva, it's time to plug in the critical branding and messaging elements. You've already defined them through your prior homework.

Start by establishing visual consistency with your color palette and logo placement. Use the exact brand colors and vector-based logo files that you have finalized rather than approximations. This ensures alignment with all other customer touchpoints like business cards and packaging.

Next, insert your tightly honed aspirational tagline in the headline placeholder, keeping it to 10 words or less. Follow up the bold promise with a paragraph calling out the precise pain points your ideal customer faces before meeting you. Quickly establish empathy and familiarity.

Further down the page, insert your three big success steps. These steps outline the transformative process your customer will undergo. Reinforce how you will guide visitors, step-by-step, to become their best selves with supportive solutions.

Finally, make your primary call-to-action button loud and proud. Use contrasting colors and action-driven text. This button should direct visitors to take their next step. They could download an offer, book a call, start a free trial, or subscribe to your email newsletter. The wireframe should emotionally resonate with your readers and move them to convert!

Step 3. Use the Completed Wireframe to Build Your Home Page

Your strategic homepage wireframe is complete. Now you're ready to build the live version on your actual website.

This is where the diligent upfront work pays off. Instead of staring at a blank webpage wondering where to start, you simply have to transpose what you've already conceptualized in your wireframe visually. It's about finding matching templates, fonts, images, colors, and content blocks. You don't have to start from scratch.

For example, website builder platforms like WordPress, Squarespace, and Wix all offer templates with similar layout structures. Drag-and-drop editors make it easy to place headlines, photos, buttons, and text sections without any coding. Modern tools empower anyone to bring their vision to life.

In the next chapter, we'll explore website hosting platforms that are best suited for personal brands. Each option comes with its own strengths and limitations, depending on your goals.

So don't worry yet about how to technically build your homepage. First, concentrate on strategic clarity. Nail your story and hero's journey first! Once your wireframe concept lands emotionally, we'll arm you with all the hosting know-how needed to make it real next.

Day 10 Exercise: Craft Your Brand Story Home Page

Let's put these homepage storyboarding concepts into action! Follow these steps:

1. Sign up for a free Canva account if you don't already have one.

2. Go to JMill.biz/wireframe to add the Wireframe Home Page Template to your Canva account.

3. Use Canva's drag-and-drop tools to map out your ideal customer journey according to your work up to this point.

4. Experiment with various photos, colors, fonts, and content arrangements. Use them to bring your ideal visitor's journey to life.

You now have an intuitive yet strategic homepage wireframe ready for implementation! In the next chapter, we'll cover translating this map into a live, lead-generating website.

Day 10 Takeaways:

- Use a wireframe template to strategically map out the key elements of your homepage before building it live. Make visitors the hero of the story.

- Establish visual brand consistency on your homepage with colors, logo, etc. Insert your aspirational tagline, address pain points, outline success steps, and add a clear call to action.

- Once your homepage wireframe resonates emotionally with your target audience, you can easily transpose it into a live website using templates. Focus on the strategic story first before technical implementation.

11

Day 11. Choose Your Website Hosting Platform

My growing online business needed a website that could keep up. But in 2014, I didn't serve more customers. Instead, I wasted hours trying to make my outdated WordPress site work by duct-taping platforms and plugins onto it. My business had evolved, and I desperately needed a better solution.

I knew there had to be a better way. A platform built specifically for people like me earning money sharing knowledge online. I was thrilled when I discovered Kajabi - one of the first end-to-end solutions for online course creators and coaches.

I migrated my whole business over that very week. Fast forward to today, and I'm still on Kajabi. I can serve more clients, produce content faster, and even enjoy weekends again now that I'm not patching things 24/7.

But Kajabi isn't the only player out there anymore. In this chapter, we'll explore today's top online platforms to find the right fit for different types of digital entrepreneurs. Whether you're a coach, author, speaker, or something else, we'll help you find what suits you.

I'll compare strengths and weaknesses to help you choose what's best for your goals and budget. The right foundation means you can stress less about logistics and deliver more value to those you serve.

Day 11. Choose Your Website Hosting Platform

WordPress powers over 60 million websites. It's undoubtedly the most used content management system. The open-source software is free, easy to use, and has a wealth of plugins and themes. So what's not to love?

While WordPress offers extreme flexibility, that can also be its downfall. The plethora of options means you must become a website developer to customize and optimize your site. And patching security vulnerabilities is an ongoing chore. Worst of all, WordPress sites tend to slow down as they grow, leading to poor page loading speeds.

For simple blogs, WordPress is perfect. But creators wanting more control over design, user experience, and monetization need a platform made for selling online courses, memberships, and services.

The 3 Best Paid Website Platforms for Online Creators

After testing the top website builders aimed at online course creators and coaches, three options stand out:

- Kajabi is the premier all-in-one platform for digital entrepreneurs. Kajabi offers elegant themes, marketing automation, and integrated payment processing. It lets you brand your site your way while handling the technical stuff behind the scenes.

- Ghost is a content management system focused on simplicity and speed. Ghost provides a streamlined backend interface and minimalist themes designed for publishing.

- Systeme is a budget-friendly alternative to Kajabi. It combines an online course builder, email marketing, and responsive website themes.

While the pricing varies widely, from $99 to $399 per month, each platform suits different needs. Let's explore the key differences.

Kajabi – The All-in-One Solution for Creatives

Kajabi is the undisputed leader for delivering premium online courses, communities, and services. The robust platform is packed with features creators need to monetize their knowledge.

With Kajabi, you can:

- Choose from dozens of sleek, professional themes and fully customize colors, fonts, and layout

- Build elegant sales funnels with landing pages, automated email sequences, and affiliate marketing

- Offer courses, memberships, downloads, and services all in one place

- Promote your brand with sophisticated email and social media marketing tools

- Manage your business and track sales in a centralized dashboard

- Expand your platform over time without the headaches of integrating multiple tools

The main downside of Kajabi is the high monthly price to get started. But when you factor in the monthly costs of all the other tools you would need to replace Kajabi, the convenience, and customization make it well worth the premium fee.

Ghost – The Better Alternative to WordPress

Ghost offers a streamlined alternative focused entirely on publishing beautiful content quickly. It also has some basic email marketing and paid membership options built in. Ghost is ideal for people who want to keep things "low-tech" and simple.

With Ghost, you can:

- Choose a simple, distraction-free theme to showcase your writing

- Write and publish posts easily from a clean, intuitive interface

- Focus on high-quality content without worrying about design or monetization

- Collect emails and send email newsletters to your list

- Create paid memberships and deliver exclusive content

- Avoid overwhelming options and technical challenges

Ghost won't work for e-commerce sites. It pairs nicely with Gumroad for creators offering smaller digital products. Keep it simple by combining Ghost for your blog with Gumroad for secure payments for your products and services.

Systeme – The All-in-One Little Brother

Systeme bills itself as the affordable alternative to Kajabi. It provides powerful online course creation and marketing features for bootstrapping entrepreneurs. It doesn't come with a steep price tag.

With Systeme, you can:

- Pick from basic but modern webpage designs and themes

- Build online courses with video hosting, quizzes, and discussion forums

- Set up email sequences, affiliate programs, and automatic webinars

- Avoid paying extra fees for bandwidth, members, or transactions

- Get started with a limited but free account

Serious course creators may outgrow Systeme's capabilities quickly. But it's a great entry-level platform for getting started with less financial risk.

Finding the Right Fit

Choosing a website platform is an important business decision. It impacts your brand, audience experience, and ability to generate revenue. Consider both your current needs and future goals.

- If you want simple and affordable, Ghost with Gumroad makes a great pairing. Focus on writing without the hassle of monetizing your site.

- If you desire an all-in-one powerhouse, Kajabi delivers the tools serious creators need. It helps them build a profitable online business. The premium price reflects the quality and depth of its features.

- If you're on a tight budget, Systeme lets you dip your toe into online courses and communities without draining your bank account. See if your business takes off before upgrading.

No platform does everything perfectly. However, understanding the strengths and limitations of these three options will set you up for long-term success online.

Day 11 Exercise: Choose Your Website Platform

Take some time to reflect on your current business needs and future goals. Make a list of the core features you need to achieve your vision. Then, compare the platforms based on must-haves versus nice-to-haves. Choosing technology that fits your business today is the smartest decision as you launch your online platform. It should also be able to scale up over time.

Day 11 Key Takeaways:

- WordPress can become slow, techy, and restrictive as your site grows

- Kajabi offers comprehensive business tools for established creators

- Ghost provides a streamlined blog for publishing content without the clutter

- Systeme is an affordable starting place for new entrepreneurs

- Evaluate your budget, needs, and goals before choosing

- Adding Gumroad lets you sell simply on any platform

12

Day 12. Create Your First Lead Magnet

When Shredded Wheat biscuits first debuted, they faced an uphill climb. The unusual pillow-shaped biscuits were tasty and wholesome. However, sales struggled for over three decades. Henry Perky realized the problem wasn't the product itself but failing to convince consumers to try it.

So Perky devised a bold giveaway - miniature cereal boxes filled with Shredded Wheat as free samples. Getting the biscuits literally into people's hands proved the key to unlocking demand. This ingenious "taste and see" marketing strategy caused sales to explode after 30 years of obscurity.[20]

Perky's creative sample boxes reveal the immense power of lead magnets for growing an audience. By offering something enticing in exchange for contact information, you convince website visitors to give you a chance. Otherwise, they might quickly move on.

Over a century after lifting Shredded Wheat out of obscurity, lead magnets remain among the most proven tools for converting strangers into engaged subscribers. This chapter reveals how to create your first lead magnet and put this age-old tactic to work, fueling your business's growth.

We'll cover the core components that go into designing irresistible lead magnets. Follow these key steps, and you, too, can craft subscriber giveaways that entice visitors to exchange their emails for your compelling content.

Day 12. Create Your First Lead Magnet

Many businesses just throw up a popup or ask visitors to subscribe with no incentive. This superficial approach rarely works. Without offering value first, people have no reason to opt in. You end up with a tiny list or buying email addresses through ads.

Asking for something without providing value comes across as self-serving. People today are bombarded with subscription offers. They've grown numb to generic requests. You need to flip the script and make it about the visitor to stand out. Lead magnets shift the focus to delivering an irresistible resource that solves a problem for your audience.

The key is to stop thinking about what you want - email addresses, sales, etc. Instead, obsess over what your audience needs. How can you make their lives better? This simple mindset shift is essential. Once you commit to overdelivering value, everything else falls into place.

Here is a proven 4-step process for creating high-converting lead magnets.

Step 1. Identify One of Your Audience's Main Struggles

Research your target audience deeply. You need to understand their world and what keeps them up at night.

Talk to real people in your audience if possible. Look for common themes in online groups. Analyze the questions they are asking. Identify their top frustrations.

Get clear on the specifics of their struggles. Don't just go with a surface-level issue. Dig deeper to find their biggest pain points.

It's like when Steve Jobs returned to Apple in the late 1990s. At first, it seemed like Apple just needed some new products to get back on track. But as Jobs dug deeper, he realized the real problem was Apple had lost its innovative soul. The company was fragmented and lacked vision. Jobs had to rebuild Apple's culture from the ground up around design and making the best products possible.

You need to be an investigative journalist digging into the real story. Keep asking why until you uncover the root of their struggles. The more painful their problems, the better. Your lead magnet can swoop in as the savior to resolve those issues.

Step 2. Design a Resource to Relieve Their Pain

Now create something that will help your audience with that core struggle. It could be a guide, checklist, resource list, video training, or template. The format matters far less than the value you deliver.

Aim to overdeliver on solutions to their biggest problems. Go above and beyond what they expect. Pack your lead magnet with as much helpful content as possible.

You might be thinking, "If I give it all away, I won't have anything to sell!"

First, you will have plenty more to teach people in your paid offerings than you think.

Second, think about a lead magnet being the aspirin and the paid product the ongoing prescription.

A lead magnet is like a sample dose of aspirin - it provides immediate relief for someone's pain point, but the effects wear off. Your paid products and coaching are more like an ongoing prescription and treatment plan from a doctor.

The aspirin sample shows people that you know how to help alleviate their headaches. It builds trust and social proof that you can provide solutions. Just like a doctor does when they provide medical advice and prescription medications for long-term health.

However, one or two aspirin can only do so much. The headache will inevitably come back until the underlying cause is addressed. That's why people seek out doctors - for an expert diagnosis, long-term treatment plan, and access to powerful medications.

Your paid products give people access to your deepest insights and expertise so they can fully solve their pain points for good. The lead magnet aspirin gives them a glimpse that more powerful solutions are available through working with you. But they need to commit to an ongoing coaching or training program to fully and permanently get rid of those headaches.

The lead magnet gets them in the door by establishing you as someone who can help. Your paid products seal the deal. They deliver lasting transformation through personal attention and access to you over time.

Step 3. Build the Delivery Mechanism

You've created an incredibly valuable resource. But the packaging matters tremendously for lead magnet success.

An intriguing title that speaks directly to the audience's struggle can pique their interest. The overview copy needs to clearly explain the benefits so they can't resist signing up.

Formatting is key. Make sure it's visually appealing and scannable with bullets, headings, and spacing. Poor design undermines perceived value.

As billionaire entrepreneur Richard Branson said, "Make something 100 people love, not 1 million people kind of like."

Lead magnets work when they delight a niche audience. So polish the delivery for your target demographic.

Include only the most essential elements on each page. Remove any fluff. Streamline the experience for fast consumption.

Finally, make sure collecting emails is seamless. Don't hide it behind a popup. Embed it elegantly into the download process. The easier you make opting in, the more leads you'll generate.

With an irresistible title, compelling copy, and easy opt-in, your lead magnet will convert visitors into subscribers all day long.

Step 4. Showcase Your Lead Magnet Prominently

The most effective place to feature your lead magnet is at the front and center of your homepage - make it obvious right in the prime "above the fold" space. You want it to catch your site visitors' attention immediately.

In addition, include links and mentions of the lead magnet in all new content you produce across channels. Add a prominently displayed signup form or link in every blog post, podcast episode, and video you publish.

You can also directly offer your lead magnet to fans on social media. For example, ask people to comment on relevant posts if they would like access to your guide, template, checklist, etc. Then DM them the link to sign up. Especially focus on connecting with followers who engage most with your content.

Finally, you can amplify your reach rapidly by testing Facebook ads targeted to your ideal customer avatar. Promote the lead magnet content itself rather than a generic ad. This allows you to quickly build an email list with those most interested in your solutions.

Mistakes That Limit Results

Here are common lead magnet mistakes to avoid:

- Creating a generic ebook with basic tips simply to capture emails

- Designing something you personally find useful instead of solving your audience's struggle

- Sloppy formatting that undermines perceived value

- Hiding it behind a popup without showing value upfront

- Promoting at the wrong time or place

Always stay laser-focused on your audience's needs and provide massive value.

Lead magnets work when they provide extreme value. Identify your audience's struggle and create something to alleviate their pain. Follow the 4-step process to develop a high-converting lead magnet. Promote it where your audience actively seeks solutions.

Day 12 Exercise: Create Your First Lead Magnet

To create your own irresistible lead magnet:

- Make a list of 3-5 challenges your audience faces

- Design 2-3 potential lead magnets to address those struggles

- Draft a title and overview for each one

- Review the drafts and select the best option

Use Canva or Google Docs to create a simple PDF. Remember, you can always improve the design later. What matters most is the valuable content.

Day 12 Key Takeaways:

- Shift to a value-first mindset focused on your audience's needs

- Follow the 4-step process: identify struggles, design a solution, polish packaging, promote at the right time and place

- Lead magnets work when they alleviate audience pain points

- Mistakes happen when the value is misaligned with the audience

- Iteration and testing are key to optimization

13

Day 13. Select Your Email List Service

I n its early days, an Atlanta startup named YesMail wanted to show off its email marketing platform. They hoped to dazzle potential customers. They decided to send a massive "opt-in" email blast to over 60 million addresses. The addresses were purchased from various databases.

The email was meant to demonstrate YesMail's delivery capacity at scale. But instead, it overwhelmed ISPs and crashed inboxes across the internet. Major news outlets reported on the "digital tidal wave." AOL temporarily blocked all emails from YesMail's domain.

This legendary email campaign became a case study in failure. It even cemented YesMail's reputation as synonymous with spam for years. [21]They learned the hard way that bigger email lists do not guarantee better results.

YesMail's epic blunder illustrates the importance of carefully selecting the right email marketing provider. This is especially important when first starting out. But by applying today's email best practices, you can transform subscriber messaging into one of your most valuable assets.

Email marketing remains one of the best tools for connecting with customers and growing a business. But to unlock its full potential, the right email platform is essential.

This chapter reveals how to select a tailored email service based on your unique needs. We won't overwhelm you with feature comparisons of different providers. Instead, we'll focus on core evaluation criteria that applies to any email partner. With the right approach, you can confidently choose a platform to take your email efforts to the next level.

Day 13. Select Your Email List Service

Let's first discuss the most common mistakes people make when first starting with email marketing.

Mistake #1. Using Gmail for Email Marketing (limited deliverability)

Many coaches, speakers, and authors often start by sending emails through their personal Gmail account. It feels easier since you already use it daily. However, Gmail caps how many emails you can send per day, throttling your ability to reach people. As you grow beyond a handful of subscribers, important messages hit spam folders. Your open rates plummet overnight.

When deliverability lags, inboxes never see your mail. Messages go straight to junk if they arrive at all. Recipients who sought your wisdom get silence instead. Engagement dies without ongoing dialogue. You lose their interest the very hour you won them.

Mistake #2. Choosing the Cheapest Option (poor deliverability)

Money matters when starting out. Many spot a deal for 100 emails at just $5 per month. Yet cut-rate services cut corners, too. Spammers flood these platforms, making big email providers block everyone as risky. Your hard-won audience vanishes without a click.

Mistake #3. Trying to Learn Complex Email Marketing Platforms

Sophisticated options baffle first-timers with fancy features. You want to craft campaigns, segment audiences, and track links. But multi-tab menus and tech vocabulary overcomplicate things. Hours pass trying to configure settings instead of creating content. Soon frustration overwhelms any progress.

Complex interfaces demand days of tutorials before sending simple newsletters. Who has time for that? It's hard enough creating content without wrestling with new software, too. You quickly lose hope that you have the chops to do this. Remember this: the simplest solution is often the best solution.

7 Questions to Ask When Choosing Your Email List Service

Selecting the right email marketing platform establishes your digital headquarters for years ahead. I've created seven vital questions that you should ask to select the right email list service. Let's review what matters most when determining where to house your subscribers.

Does it have good email deliverability?

Deliverability makes or breaks your outreach. Stick with email list services known for over 90% inbox placement. Publishers release reports every year on the latest deliverability rates for each provider.

Later, I'll share with you my top four providers that meet this criteria.

Does it offer email marketing automation?

You want to avoid getting overwhelmed with automation at first. However, it's still a good idea to have some automation. For example, a simple automated email is important. It delivers your lead magnet or welcomes new subscribers. Automation allows you to scale your business and influence. Just know some free plans exclude these features.

Does it allow tagging or segmenting subscribers?

While you may not need it at the very beginning, segmenting your list over time is a smart move. It sets you up for future success as your email list grows.

The words "tagging" or "segmenting" essentially mean the same thing. The concept is about placing your subscribers into small buckets based on their interests.

For example, let's say I send an email that gives away a free PDF checklist on how to write a book. I can set up a simple automation if my email list service offers segmenting.

I can create an automated setting to add a tag to anyone who clicks on that link in my email. I could also name the tag "aspiring authors."

By tagging my list, I can send more relevant emails to certain subscribers. I could send the "aspiring authors" tag emails about my book writing course. This is how you can make more sales without burning out your list.

How does their price compare?

While pricing does matter, keep in mind you often get what you pay for. Just because it is free doesn't mean it is the best option.

For example, some free email list providers do not include automation. Lacking automation makes it difficult to build an email list. One of the best ways to build your list is to give away a free PDF, also called a lead magnet. To deliver that lead magnet automatically, you need access to automation tools.

Do they offer easy landing pages?

Back when I first started, you had to pay separately for landing page software and an email list-building tool. On top of that, you had to figure out how to get them to work together nicely. Today, most email list services offer built-in landing pages.

Landing pages are important because these are the web pages you share to get people to opt-in to your list. Make sure your email list service has landing pages as one of the core features.

Is the user interface easy to use?

Not all email list services are alike. Some are simpler to use than others. At the very basic level, you need to know how to send a broadcast email to your list. Beyond that, learning how to create an automated email sequence is important too.

Later, I will share with you the four best email list services. Each of them also has easy-to-use interfaces.

Is quality technical support available?

Make sure the service you choose offers live chat if at all possible. This is important if you are having trouble sending emails or if something goes wrong. Live chat support has saved the day for me more than once whenever I was in the middle of a big launch.

The 4 Best Email List Services for Authors, Coaches, and Speakers

Now, let's talk about my four favorite email list services that meet all of the criteria I mentioned earlier. Features and tools are always changing, but at the time of writing this chapter, here are my favorites (in no certain order).

Option 1. ConvertKit

ConvertKit offers strong automation with its email marketing. Even those on the free plan enjoy unlimited landing pages, forms, and broadcast capabilities. The only limitation is access to pre-built email sequences, which requires an upgrade.

However, the free "Forever" plan still allows up to 1,000 subscribers, which provides ample room to grow. Unlimited broadcasting means you can send new content regularly without worrying about caps.

Prices remain cost-effective for premium features like welcome flows and email courses. And subscribers can go into the tens of thousands before bumping pricing tiers. ConvertKit has excellent deliverability and strong reviews. It is an ideal starting place for creators who want to nurture a following through automated email marketing.

Option 2. MailerLite

The free version of MailerLite also caps at 1,000 subscribers, offering creators plenty of capacity initially. The biggest draw comes from their open Automation Builder. It's available even on free accounts, allowing welcome emails and other messaging sequences.

While capped at only 12,000 emails per month for the first 1,000 fans, that may suit those focused on high-quality over high-quantity interactions. For example, in many cases, weekly broadcast emails would still keep you well under that monthly limit.

In summary, MailerLite brings intuitive automation without paying extra fees. ConvertKit has some advantages in reviews and ratings for email deliverability. However, MailerLite compares well in key free offering criteria. For some, especially with tight startup budgets, MailerLite deserves consideration as an email marketing launch pad.

Option 3. Systeme.io

Systeme combines an all-in-one online business platform with built-in email marketing. For those wanting an integrated experience, Systeme provides deep functionality. It covers e-commerce, landing pages, and email. Their editor simplifies the creation of nicely designed newsletters and promotional emails.

On basic plans, Systeme caps marketing emails to 1,000 prospects per month. Upgrades substantially grow capacity while remaining affordable. They compete well with users who want marketing, sales, and email unified under one roof. This is because of their quality ratings and transparent pricing. Consider Systeme to broaden your capabilities on your entrepreneurial journey.

Option 4. Kajabi (My personal favorite)

Kajabi functions like Systeme. It's an integrated platform for online courses, email marketing, and other core business needs. It earns high marks and is my personal top choice.

Kajabi specifically helps segment engaged email subscribers. You can then send them targeted promotions, offers, and subscriber journeys related to your niche. Expect stellar deliverability from industry leaders. Kajabi also offers award-winning support teams available via live chat.

Day 13 Exercise: Select Your Email List Service

Finding an email marketing sidekick to grow your community doesn't need overthinking. With just Internet access and 10 minutes, you can identify the perfect match.

First, write down your top priority for a provider - is it price, ease of use, features, or deliverability? Circle the one aspect most critical for you.

Next, reread the four options I mentioned earlier to determine which one best fits your priorities.

Finally, sign up for a free trial. All four options (ConvertKit, Mailer-Lite, Systeme, and Kajabi) either have a limited free trial or a forever free option. Test sending a newsletter, creating a landing page, or even setting up an automated welcome email for new subscribers.

If you are satisfied during a trial run, wonderful! You found a solution that can work for you. If not, simply try another until you find the one that works best for you.

Day 13 Key Takeaways:

• Select a specialist provider, don't rely on personal accounts.

• Prioritize 95%+ deliverability. Leads mean nothing if emails hit spam.

• Start with free plans, allowing essentials like subscribers, templates, and automation.

14

Day 14. Design the Perfect Landing Page

A hilarious 90-second video was the only thing on the otherwise blank webpage. The video doesn't have elaborate graphics or sales messages. It just has a wacky spokesperson pitching budget-friendly razors. The page looked ridiculously simple. This was especially true for a company trying to wrestle market share from the behemoth Gillette.

But that single landing page with the funny video was magic. Within 48 hours, Dollar Shave Club had over 12,000 subscribers who couldn't wait to get their hands on these affordable razors. Practically overnight, an upstart landed major venture capital funding to the tune of $1 million. Just two years after launch, Unilever acquired Dollar Shave Club for a cool $1 billion.[22]

The runaway success of Dollar Shave Club dramatically shows the immense power of a dedicated landing page. Unlike homepages bogged down with navigation links and competing calls-to-action, Dollar Shave Club's one-page approach compelled visitors to subscribe.

This chapter will reveal how to craft high-converting landing pages. It will show you how to turn website visitors into leads, sales, and loyal followers. By focusing each page on one compelling offer instead of sending visitors to a generic homepage, you'll see conversions skyrocket.

Day 14. Design the Perfect Landing Page

Many businesses make the mistake of sending website visitors to their home pages without clear calls to action. They pour money into driving visitors, expecting their generic homepage will somehow magically convert visitors into leads and sales.

But miscellaneous company homepages fail miserably when it comes to conversions. These generic pages showcase services, provide contact info and try to welcome all audiences. Without a singular focus, homepages confuse visitors. They have an overload of navigation links vying for attention.

Your homepage traffic floods into the Bermuda Triangle, never to be seen again. Few visitors will take the initiative to poke around your services or offerings without some direction.

Many times, website visitors scan for something relevant and, finding nothing of interest, quickly bounce to another site. Those visitors are lost with almost no chance of return.

Instead, your landing page should have one purpose. It is to get visitors to take one specific action, like downloading a lead magnet or signing up for a free trial.

Sending visitors to dedicated landing pages can improve conversion rates. They can reach 50% or higher when done correctly. To reach these kinds of conversion rates, follow these five best practices.

Step 1. Craft an Irresistible Headline

Your headline is the first thing visitors see on your landing page. An effective headline convinces visitors to keep reading and take action. Follow these tips for writing high-converting headlines:

- Clearly state the benefit the visitor will receive from taking action. For example: "Get My Free Guide to Launching a Successful Blog."

- Use emotional words like "discover," "avoid," and "create" to trigger desire.

- Utilize the list headline formula: "10 Ways to..."

- Keep headlines short and scannable, ideally 6-10 words.

- Test different headlines and see which converts best. The right headline can double conversions.

Remember, your headline should provide visitors with a compelling reason to opt-in to your offer.

Step 2. Showcase a Productized Lead Magnet

Visitors are more likely to opt in when they can visualize the lead magnet. Use images and graphics to showcase your offer as an appealing product. Here are some tips for productizing your lead magnet:

- Mock up the lead magnet with a realistic product image. Canva provides templates.

- Make it resemble a physical product with textures and shadows.

- Show it on a phone, computer screen, or other context.

- Feature your brand logo and visual identity.

Productized lead magnets boost perceived value and conversions by up to 30%.

Step 3. Drive Action with the CTA Button

The call-to-action button prompts visitors to opt-in to your lead magnet. By default, most buttons have the text "submit" or "subscribe." You will want to change the text on your call-to-action buttons in order to increase your conversion rate. An effective CTA compels visitors to click by sharing some type of benefit.

Follow these CTA button best practices:

- Use benefit-focused action words like "Download Now" or "Get Instant Access."

- Make the button large and high-contrast with bright colors.

- Place the button at the top part of the page so it can be seen without scrolling down.

- Limit forms to 1-2 fields like name and email address.

- Test different button text, colors, and sizes for the best conversion rate.

Optimizing your CTA button can lift conversions by 10-15%. The right call to action makes opting in irresistible.

Step 4. Streamline with a One-Page Approach

Online attention spans average just 8 seconds. A cluttered landing page hinders conversions. A focused one-page approach removes distractions.

Here's how to streamline your landing page:

- Eliminate main navigation links as well as footer links.

- Hide ads, widgets, videos, and other clutter.

- Stick to one background image or solid color.

- Use plenty of white space for a clean layout.

- Keep page length short by removing secondary content.

- Ensure the page loads quickly—under 2 seconds.

By minimizing distractions, a streamlined one-page approach can double conversion rates.

Step 5. Boost Credibility with Social Proof

First-time visitors are skeptical of opting in. Reassure them by showcasing social proof of your expertise and credibility.

Effective types of social proof include:

- Testimonials describing amazing benefits from your content.

- Logos of featured brands and publications.

- Number of subscribers, downloads, or sales.

- Awards and media features.

Subtly integrating 2-3 elements lifts conversions by 15% on average. But avoid overusing social proof, as that looks desperate.

Pro Tip: Use Exit-Intent Popups

Want to grab visitors who are about to leave your landing page? Use exit-intent popups to offer lead magnets to potential abandoning visitors. Studies show exit-intent popups can capture 70% of abandoning visitors and increase overall conversions by up to 25%.

Common Landing Page Mistakes to Avoid

While the strategies above set you up for success, there are a few common mistakes that can sabotage your landing page:

- Using stock photos that don't connect with your target audience

- Neglecting your page copy and focusing just on the opt-in form

- Making your page too salesy instead of benefit-focused

- Cluttering your page with too many images, links, videos, or text blocks

By being aware of these missteps, you can craft landing pages that generate maximum leads.

Creating a high-converting landing page is crucial for driving leads and sales from your online marketing. Follow the strategic principles in this chapter. For example, showcase a productized lead magnet and use a benefit-focused headline. This will make conversion rates skyrocket.

Day 14 Exercise: Design Your Perfect Landing Page

Here is a 10-15 minute landing page design exercise:

Step 1. Identify Your Offer (2-3 min). Come up with a free offer or lead magnet you will provide in exchange for a website visitor's email address. Summarize the offer and key benefit in 1-2 sentences.

Step 2. Craft Your Headline (2-3 min). Write a compelling, emotional headline that clearly communicates the main benefit of your offer. Aim for 6-10 words.

Step 3. Describe Your CTA Button (1-2 min). Describe the main call-to-action button to access your offer. Use benefit-driven text for your buttons like "download, get access, or start here.

Step 4. Pick a Social Proof Element (1-2 min). Choose a type of social proof to include on your page, such as testimonials, logos, or subscriber numbers.

Step 5. Sketch the Landing Page Layout (3-5 min). Sketch the layout of your landing page on paper, including elements like the headline, offer image, opt-in form, CTA button, and social proof.

Day 14 Key Takeaways:

- Focus landing pages on one offer and call to action

- Craft compelling headlines focused on visitor benefits

- Productize your lead magnet with professional graphics

- Use high-contrast CTAs with action-focused language

- Streamline pages by removing navigation links and clutter

- Add social proof elements to build visitor trust

15

Day 15. Set Up Your Automated Prospect Funnel

Two brothers ran a humble but efficient burger and milkshake restaurant in the 1950s in San Bernardino, California. Customers loved the convenient walk-up windows and hearty, affordable meals served in a few minutes. Yet despite its popularity with locals, expanding reach seemed unlikely for this small standalone restaurant.

Enter Ray Kroc - a hardworking salesman who saw much bigger potential. He became fascinated by the restaurant's smooth product flow. So, he convinced the founders to franchise the concept. He then developed rigorous operating standards, ensuring perfectly consistent customer experiences. Disciplined systems enable automated cooking and purchasing. This allowed regular employees to deliver the quality people expected.

The same insight applies to digital sales. You need simple, automated systems to create freedom in your personal brand business. The right automated relationship-building sequences let ordinary experts scale their businesses. This is like how Kroc turned a local walkup eatery into a global empire known as McDonald's.[23]

This strategy shows how to turn strangers into enthusiastic clients. It does this through personalized messaging that works for you 24/7. Master this skill once, then profit from inbound interest for years hands-free. Use technology to focus on your genius zone while nurturing followers into your perfect customers.

Day 15. Set Up Your Automated Prospect Funnel

So you just created your author website or set up an online coaching business. Awesome! But now what? You see your elegant homepage and neat social media profiles. You are eager to get started. But your excitement fades as a little nervousness sets in. How do you actually start attracting your ideal prospects?

Most hopeful entrepreneurs drop links to their new online homes through social channels. Click here to download my free book! Go to my site and sign up for a newsletter! Check out my life-changing coaching services! This spray-and-pray approach is understandable - you worked hard on that website and want to get some clicks. But randomly posting links typically leads nowhere.

The problem is randomly sharing your links fails to build real relationships. Sure, Aunt Martha and your college roommate Dan might click over and encourage you. But visitors will come and go without a way to follow up or nurture possible leads. No one knows or trusts this random online expert telling them to opt in or buy something. You remain alone on your island, hoping a plane of prospects flies over and lands somehow.

Yet many solopreneurs still avoid using opt-in forms, email lists, or anything that seems too "salesy." We just want people to show up and buy stuff naturally, right? But, building real influence means carefully bringing strangers closer. It's an intentional process over time. There are no shortcuts. But what should that process actually look like? The best way to get started is to implement the following three steps.

Step 1: Create Your First Lead Magnet

It all starts with capturing attention. The irresistible lead magnet offers a way for visitors to become subscribers. This free PDF checklist, audio training, or other giveaway acts as the cornerstone for building your automated funnel. But what makes for good lead magnet ideas exactly?

First, remember the goal is to acquire email addresses from qualified leads. Your perfect reader stumbles upon your homepage or social media. They wonder who you are and if you can actually help them. Then, this attractive action step pops out, allowing an easy, risk-free gateway into your world.

Simplicity wins. Focus first on furthering the relationship, not getting a sale. Because, again, that eventual conversion can only happen after building familiarity and trust over time. This freebie is merely the hook to begin meaningful follow-up communication.

Now crafting the right irresistible "hook" requires knowing your fish in this analogy. Attempting mass appeal almost always backfires for solopreneurs. Instead, define one ultra-specific reader avatar and create messages solely for this niche. Use the avatar's age, gender, income level, frustrations, and goals to help you come up with a great lead magnet.

For example, Ruth is a 42-year-old suburban mom earning $60k a year with two kids. After chaotic days, she dreams of getting fit again but lacks money and energy. Offer a lead magnet like "How Busy Moms Can Finally Lose 10 Pounds In 6 Weeks" to capture her opt-in. This hyper-focused relevance pulls in qualified contacts. They are actually interested in the solutions you provide.

Step 2: Set Up Your Automated Welcome Email

Someone just opted in to download your lead magnet. The automation has begun! But don't leave new contacts hanging in awkward virtual silence, wondering what happens next. Remember those crucial first few minutes after an introduction? Handshakes, eye contact, and quick rapport building?

Treat your new digital subscribers the same way. Send them an immediate, personalized welcome email. This simple message serves three important relationship growth functions:

1. It Keeps Your Word

You promoted some exclusive incentive content in exchange for an email address. Hold up your end of this value-for-information bargain right away. Send newcomers straight to that awesome resource keeping implied promises.

2. It Makes Them Feel Special

That lead magnet really resonated with their inner hopes. Let your invitee know you recognize and appreciate their wise decision by welcoming them into your community. A little praise and recognition go a long way, especially early on.

3. It Primes Next Steps

What an opportunity knocking now! Your warmest followers landed directly inside your email list. Seize this engaged momentum and point them where to go next. Maybe it's booking a call, checking a blog, or visiting a certain page. Lead gently towards rising action.

Step 3. Create Your Automated Follow-Up Sequence

You hooked interest with the lead magnet and set expectations with an automated welcome message. Traffic and opt-ins grow. Now what? The fate of your funnel rests completely upon what happens next in this fragile relationship-building phase.

Many well-intentioned solopreneurs push new contacts too hard for a sale. They do this right after the acquisition. But prospects need time and reason to trust your ability actually to help them. According to marketing data compiled by Dean Jackson, 85% of subscribers buy something after 90 days of being on your list.

That doesn't mean you shouldn't offer anything for sale in the first 90 days. It means you need to have a long-term view of your email list. Focus on value in your automated sequences. So what should a core follow-up series contain specifically? Here are some of my personal favorite follow-up emails.

Day 1: The "How Can I Help" Email

Ask how the lead magnet is working for them so far. Offer live support via booking a call or providing contact info for questions.

Day 3: The "My #1 Tip" Email

Share your absolute best business or life strategy. Then tie its value to signing up for coaching or a program.

Day 5: The "Goodbye, Hello" Email

Recap how you met initially. Introduce yourself again by sharing your personal journey. Talk about all the things your subscriber can say goodbye to once they've reached their goal. Also, tie in all the new, exciting things they can say hello to once they reach their goal. Then, tie in how your coaching or course can help them close the gap from where they are to where they want to be.

Day 7: The "Big Benefit" Email

Describe the tangible transformation your services make possible. Frame your features as benefits, solving their pain points. Extend an offer to help by way of your coaching or courses.

Use these proven templates early. Then, keep adding unique value for months and years. Well-timed, personalized outreach will turn cold prospects into satisfied customers. This outreach, combined with free evergreen training content, does the trick.

BONUS: The "Private Invite" Email

I have a Swiss Army knife email that I use quite frequently. This special email aims to attract new coaching clients from your current email list. I call it the "private invite email." The email speaks directly to prospects who know and trust you. You let them know that you are opening up x number of spots in your coaching program starting sometime this month. You let them know the specific goal you have in mind for this opportunity (examples include writing a book, creating an online course, etc.). Then, invite them to reply to the email if they are interested, and you'll send along some more information.

This tactful private nudge gauges buyer readiness while reaffirming ongoing helpfulness. It can turn previous list members into new coaching clients. This is thanks to personalization combined with opportunity.

Send these one-on-one private invites regularly. Sprinkle them randomly among other broadcasts. With familiarity and scarcity as leverage, this email consistently yields new coaching leads over time.

Day 15 Exercise: Draft Your Automated Follow-Up Sequence

This exercise will help you start creating good follow-up messages. They will help you nurture new contacts into loyal followers.

1. **Identify Your Ideal Reader Avatar.** Focus your efforts on helping a very specific type of customer. Jot down the goals, passions, and struggles they face daily.

2. **Write Your Day 1 "How Can I Help" Email.** Ask sincere questions about how your lead magnet resource is working for them so far. Provide your contact info and availability for live support too.

3. **Compose Your Day 3 "My #1 Tip" Email.** Genuinely share your single best business or life lesson. Relate its usefulness to whatever solution - coaching program or product - you provide next at their self-directed pace.

4. **Draft a Day 5 "Goodbye, Hello" Email.** Reintroduce yourself and your own transformational journey. Discuss opportunities to leave pain points behind and embrace exciting progress through your services.

Follow this blueprint to turn cold traffic into committed brand advocates. Nurture trust by serving needs long-term until buyers are ready.

Day 15 Key Takeaways:

• Create a high-value lead magnet to capture ideal prospect contacts

• Welcome and deliver promises promptly after opt-in

• Nurture leads consistently with value, no sales pitches

• Embrace automated funnels for scalable client growth

16

Day 16. Create Your About Me Page

B enjamin Franklin's Autobiography is considered one of the most influential works in early American literature. The book was published in 1791 when Franklin was 84 years old. It chronicles his life from humble beginnings as the son of a candlemaker. It follows his rise as a successful printer, inventor, Founding Father, and diplomat.

What made Franklin's autobiography so memorable was his engaging, conversational style. He wrote it not merely to catalog his achievements but to connect with readers by sharing the story of his life. Franklin took them along on the journey from poverty to prosperity, discussing his mistakes and lessons learned along the way.

The Autobiography inspired many future American writers. It provided an early model for using narrative to share one's experience.

In that same engaging spirit, this chapter will explore how to craft an "about me" page. It won't just list credentials. Rather, it will draw readers in by introducing yourself through a compelling life story.

The goal is not to brag but to connect. Much like Benjamin Franklin's famous work, opening up makes the "about me" page more inviting.[24]

Day 16. Create Your About Me Page

When creating an "About Me" page, it's tempting just to list your achievements and credentials. However, this formal, achievement-focused approach often fails to connect with visitors.

Many people mistakenly believe the page is all about them. Visitors care less about your accomplishments and more about what you can do for them. They want to know if you understand their struggles and can provide solutions. An "About Me" page that is overly focused on achievements and credentials is self-centered. It should be visitor-centered.

Some common pitfalls include making it too much of an academic biography. Others are using stiff, formal language or being boring by rattling off credentials. This fails to engage readers. They want a glimpse into the real human behind the website, not just a laundry list of degrees and job titles.

The most effective approach is keeping the focus on visitors' needs instead of yourself. Introduce who you are briefly, but mainly explain how you can connect with and assist readers. Share your guiding principles and what drives you to help others overcome challenges. Use your story to forge a bond, not just spotlight yourself. The "About Me" page shouldn't be about you at all—it should be about them.

Step 1. Craft an Introduction That Draws Readers In

Your "About Me" page introduction is a lot like a first date—you want to make a great first impression. This means not dominating the conversation by bragging about yourself but keeping the focus on getting to know the other person.

A good analogy is to approach your introduction like you would a first date. Don't just list your job titles or rattle off achievements. Reveal your personality. Share your passions, quirks, and beliefs. Tell a story from your past that shaped you. Help visitors get to know the real human behind the website right away.

Introduce yourself briefly to establish credibility. For example, mention your role as an author, blogger, coach, or expert in your field. But don't dwell on accomplishments. Quickly pivot to show you understand visitors' needs, worries, and desires. Reflecting their own thoughts back at readers establishes rapport quickly.

Craft your opening to hint at the journey ahead if visitors stay on your site. You're offering to be their guide, but they need to know you can truly empathize with their problems first. Remember, first impressions matter. Use your introduction to connect with visitors, not just sell yourself immediately.

Step 2. Identify and Empathize with Visitors' Struggles

Once you've introduced yourself, the next step is crucial. It involves identifying and empathizing with your visitors' struggles.

In Uncle Tom's Cabin, Harriet Beecher Stowe masterfully portrayed slaves' pain and desperation. She did this through vivid portraits. Her novel deeply resonated by illuminating an experience unfamiliar to many readers at the time. She connected by conveying how much the slaves were suffering.

On your "About Me" page, strive to tap into your audience's mindset by articulating familiar pains, doubts, and concerns. List out quotes and phrases your readers may think or say. For example:

"I'm full of ideas but can't seem to start."

"I'm tired of staying stuck in this dead-end job."

"What if I'm not good enough?"

By giving voice to these inner worries and fears, you show visitors that you deeply understand where they are coming from. You can then position yourself as the guide who relates to their distress and wants to help them overcome it. But first, show you truly get what they're going through. When readers see their own thoughts mirrored back, it powerfully communicates that you grasp their situation.

Step 3. Guide Visitors to Solve Struggles

Once you've established empathy with your readers' pain points, the next step is explaining how you can guide them to solve those struggles.

According to a study, including testimonials on a website increased the likelihood of purchases by 34%. This is because it builds visitor trust by providing social proof that you deliver results.

On your "About Me" page, highlight specific ways you've helped people overcome the same challenges plaguing your readers. For example:

"I helped Julie finally quit her unfulfilling office job and open her own bakery."

"I worked with Mark to create a focused writing routine so he could finish his novel."

"My coaching enabled Sandra to find the courage to speak up in meetings and be heard."

Back up your expertise with evidence. Share case studies, client reviews, testimonials, or examples of your work in action. Prove that you've assisted others on the same journey your visitors want to undertake.

Remember, your goal is to guide—so provide a roadmap for how you can help readers make progress. Outline your method, framework, or system. Explain your distinct approach to serving clients. Clarify what makes you uniquely qualified to assist visitors in conquering their difficulties. Convince readers you offer a clear path forward.

Step 4. Establish Credibility

Once you've explained how you can help visitors overcome struggles, the next step is establishing your credibility. As Mark Twain stated, "The man who does not read has no advantage over the man who cannot read." Credentials matter when it comes to consulting someone for help.

Briefly highlight your background. Explain your relevant experience that makes you qualified to serve readers. For example, mention if you:

- Have an advanced degree in your field

- Completed specialized training or certifications

- Authored books or courses on this topic

- Have been featured as an expert on major media platforms

- Have accrued years of successfully coaching clients like the reader

Displaying logos of publications, podcasts, or websites where you've been featured or quoted is also powerful social proof. Visitors want reassurance you have the expertise to guide them.

While credentials are crucial, resist solely resorting to listing qualifications. Sprinkle in just enough biographical details to substantiate your authority. The focus is on quickly convincing readers you are qualified to help them, not an in-depth overview of your career progression. A few key credentials strategically placed establish credibility so readers see you as an expert they can trust.

Step 5. End with a Clear Call to Action

After establishing your expertise, conclude your "About Me" page by directing visitors to take the next step.

Legend tells of sirens luring sailors to shipwrecks through irresistible songs. Their melodies compelled men to action. End your page in a similar way. Urge readers to take clear action. This could mean signing up for a newsletter, scheduling a consultation, or downloading a resource.

Close by motivating visitors to convert from browsing to buying into your guidance. For example:

"Ready to stop wasting time and start accomplishing your goals? Click here to download my free guide on building an effective morning routine."

Or "Want me to personally help clarify your business mission? Schedule a 1-on-1 coaching session now."

Direct readers to take a concrete next action. You want your message to be so compelling that visitors feel urged to click. An explicit call to conversion completes the journey you've outlined.

Start your "About Me" page with a strong opening. Follow this with an empathetic middle, social proof, and established credentials. Finally, end by giving readers a clear avenue to get started on achieving their aspirations. Send visitors off with a siren song they just can't resist.

Day 16 Exercise: Write a Draft of Your About Me Page

To start applying these lessons on an "About Me" page that truly connects, set aside 10 minutes to complete this quick exercise:

1. Write down the core struggles your readers face. What pains and frustrations keep them up at night? Really get inside their heads.

2. Next, explain how you can help guide them past those struggles. What solutions, insights, or tools can you provide to help overcome their challenges?

3. Craft an introduction that draws readers in. Begin by briefly introducing yourself. Then, shift focus to empathizing with their situation.

4. End with an irresistible call to action for signing up for more of your guidance. Make it so compelling that visitors cannot say no.

Invest just 10 minutes in practicing connecting with your audience's needs. Write down their struggles, the value you offer, and a strong opening and closing. This will give you greater clarity before sitting down to write your full "About Me" page. Ensuring you are truly visitor-focused instead of self-focused is the key takeaway.

Completing this quick exercise will help you master the strategies shared in this chapter for an "About Me" page that truly resonates. The goal is not to boast about yourself but to forge a bond with readers. So set your timer for 10 minutes and start connecting your story to the people you want to help!

Day 16 Key Takeaways:

- Focus on connecting with and helping readers, not yourself.

- Draw readers in, address their concerns, and share solutions.

- Establish expertise but don't overdo credentials.

- End with a clear call to action.

- Craft engaging opening and closing to compel readers.

17

Day 17. Create Your Work with Me Page

Inside every Apple store, a literal "Work With Me" Genius Bar takes center stage. This prominent bar-style counter displays signage clearly listing one-on-one tech support services. They cover everything from device set-up to data migration. And the prices are transparent.

Customers can also easily book appointments. You can use them for personalized troubleshooting or lessons tailored to your needs.

This easy access to Apple's expertise has driven over $5 billion in annual service revenue. The Genius Bar removes obstacles. It builds trust at the start of customer relationships.[25]

Just like Apple, your website can feature an effective Work With Me page that broadcasts your expertise. You should detail your coaching packages, availability, and pricing.

This helps ideal prospects find and buy personalized support. They can use it to get "unstuck" or to reach new goals.

The story of Apple's Genius Bar carries an important lesson - people want transformation, not just information. By implementing the guidance in this chapter, you'll have your own revenue-generating "Genius Bar."

Day 17. Create Your Work with Me Page

Many people trying to build an audience lack a dedicated page clearly explaining how to work with them. Information about services and pricing gets scattered across their sites or left out completely. This confusion frustrates potential customers.

Why doesn't this approach work? People won't commit to something they don't fully understand. You must provide clear explanations of the offer. This will help potential clients make informed decisions.

Some common mistakes include:

- not listing prices upfront

- only showcasing the most expensive service

- using vague language to describe offerings

- and hiding the Work With Me page deep in a confusing website.

Instead, be very specific on one page about exactly what you provide and what it costs. Detail every service offering and pricing tier clearly. Make it easy for ideal clients to find and comprehend key information. Removing friction leads to more bookings. Clarity helps buyers understand quickly if you meet their needs.

Why You Should Create a Work with Me Page

There are a few key reasons why launching right away with a dedicated Work With Me page is so valuable.

First, It's an easy way to get started. A Work With Me page only takes about an hour to set up using an existing template. Then, your services and offerings are visible, and you're open for business.

Second, It's versatile. This type of coaching/services page works for those operating in any industry niche. Whether you specialize in relationships, finance, marketing, or something else, a Work With Me page can work in almost any industry.

Third, It attracts ideal clientele. Detailing your coaching packages and pricing demonstrates clearly who you aim to serve. Those intrigued and able to invest in such offerings will self-select and connect with you through your Work With Me page.

Launching right off the bat with a dedicated Work With Me page makes starting your platform simple. It broadcasts what you do. It puts the ideal next steps for committed, high-end clients to find and act on. This facilitates growth and speeds up your ability to start working with your best-fit audience.

The Two Work with Me Models: Talk-First vs Pay-First

When creating a Work With Me page, you must decide which of two main models to use.

Talk-First Pages

The "Talk-First" model leads with an application or booking flow first before any pricing or packages are presented. Site visitors are asked to fill out some information and schedule a call with you before purchasing services.

This allows you to qualify leads. It ensures alignment through a conversation before finalizing a coaching engagement. It avoids prematurely selling services.

Pay-First Pages

"Pay-First" pages show the pricing, packages, and investment details upfront. They come before any application or scheduling step. This allows site visitors to view services and rates first and then purchase and schedule if they feel ready.

The benefit here is capturing buyers who already know your offerings resonate and are ready to commit. The tradeoff is potentially attracting clients who are not a good fit for what you do.

Talk-First pages enable conversational qualification, while Pay-First pages enable spontaneous purchases. Consider your niche, offerings, and target client mindset. Use this info when deciding which model could best optimize your conversion funnel. Now, let's take a closer look at both models.

Option 1. Creating an Effective Talk-First Page

If you decide the "Talk-First" model is best for your business, here are some tips for making an effective, application-focused Work With Me page:

Lead With a Value-Driven Headline

Capture attention with a compelling headline focused on the value you provide - not just the services you offer. Communicate the transformation you help facilitate.

Include an Explanatory Video

A short 1-3 minute video further detailing who you help, their struggles, and how you can guide them can communicate empathy and build trust.

Use an Engaging Lead Gen Form

Ask site visitors to share a bit about goals and challenges before a call. This will set up the call and ensure it is worth everyone's time to connect further.

Ask Three Qualifying Application Questions

To avoid overloading applicants, use just 2-3 focused questions tailored to your niche and offer. I use three tailored questions. They assess commitment, coaching readiness, and financial ability. You will need to adjust these questions to fit the outcomes you help people achieve. Here are my favorite three types of application questions.

Question 1. The Commitment Question

By asking site visitors to rate their commitment (on a scale of 1-5) to the outcome you help people achieve, you immediately qualify their level of dedication and mindset. This ensures you don't waste time with the uncommitted. Here's how I state the commitment question along with the multiple-choice answers.

On a scale of 1-5, how committed are you to growing your business?

- *1 – Not much*

- *2 – Just curious*

- *3 – It's a "someday" thing for sure*

- *4 – Pretty motivated*

- *5 – Super motivated!*

Question 2. The Coaching Readiness Question

Gauging openness to receiving support and being coached also assesses willingness to invest in guidance. Response scores signal fit with your collaborative process. Here's how I state the coaching readiness question along with the multiple-choice answers.

On a scale of 1-5, how open are you to receiving support and being coached to your next level of success?

- *1 – I can be stuck in my ways*

- *2 – Open, but not sure an online business is what I want*

- *3 – I'm open and willing to learn*

- *4 – I'm very open and tired of doing this on my own*

- *5 – I'm super open and ready to take action on what you tell me to do next*

Question 3. The Financial Ability Question

Lastly, asking directly about someone's ability to devote time, money, and effort shows if they have the needed resources. You weed out window shoppers. Here's how I state the ability & means question along with the multiple-choice answers.

On a scale of 1-5, how willing are you to invest time, money, and energy in building your online business?

- *1 – Not at all (at this time)*

- *2 – I have little time and resources, but not looking to invest them in building my business right now*

- *3 – I have access to the financial resources to invest in building my online business*

- *4 – I have the ability to invest in building my online business, and it's a priority for me*

- *5 – I'm ready to invest and motivated to back it up with time and energy (ready to make it happen)!*

These three application questions help decide if a good match and opportunity exist. They do this by comparing commitment, coachability, work ethic, and budget. They minimize fruitless consultations and maximize reciprocal value.

In summary, lead with value rather than product details. Qualify demand proactively. Use a tailored application sequence before asking for payment or commitment. Guide site visitors through small commitments. These help make good matches and set up fruitful consultations for both parties.

Option 2. Creating a High-Converting Pay-First Page

If you decide that a "Pay-First" model is best for quickly monetizing your expertise and coaching, here are some tips for making an optimized page:

Lead with a strong headline. Start with a catchy headline. It should explain the real benefits a client will get from working with you.

Show your pricing prominently. Show pricing tiers and packages upfront. They should have clear service details, not vague ideas.

Offer multiple buying options. In addition to an intro session, you can also offer month-long or quarterly coaching packages. They are for those seeking longer-term support on their growth journey.

Create outcome-driven names for your coaching packages. Descriptive package names let site visitors identify with them. The names of the coaching packages should match their aspirations. For example, those seeking "The Transformation Track" or "The Breakthrough Bundle."

Reassure with credibility elements. Include testimonials. Also, use social proof or media features. They help to establish authority and trust for your premium-priced services.

Simplify the scheduling process. Integrate scheduling software. Payments will then seamlessly lead to booking. They will not need to take any further steps.

Communicate serious value quickly. Promote pricing proudly. Facilitate ongoing support. Provide social proof. And make the next steps easy. These steps maximize conversions of those already compelled by your offering enough to pay upfront.

Day 17 Exercise: Create Your Work with Me Page Draft

After reading about the pros and cons of both Talk-First and Pay-First Work With Me pages, the next step is to spend 10-15 minutes drafting your own. This will help you see which model fits your coaching approach and audience.

To begin, open up a blank document or notebook to use for outlining and brainstorming. Set a timer for 5 minutes. During this time, sketch the basic parts of your Work With Me page. Craft an intriguing headline that speaks to the changes you cultivate. Then, choose if you want to lead with an application flow (Talk-First) or showcase pricing and packages first (Pay-First).

If going the Pay-First route, jot down ideas for three creative coaching package names along with potential pricing. If you like the Talk-First approach, draft three tailored application questions. You want prospects to answer them before booking a call. Use the examples about assessing readiness as a guide.

After 5 minutes of initial outlining, set another timer for 5-10 additional minutes. Look at your rough sketch. Flesh out the ideas by writing 1-2 paragraphs for each section. Describe your packages or explain your application questions. Write freely, getting clear on the details.

Once the timer goes off, review what you have created. Which model does your draft lean towards? Do the listed offerings and questions reflect your niche? Do they reflect your position and ideal client? Would a prospective reader clearly understand the next steps you are asking them to take?

This quick DIY exercise of prototyping your own Work With Me page reveals useful insights. Use this as a starting point. Then, use the advice in this chapter to make a page that converts visitors into coaching clients.

Day 17 Key Takeaways:

- Create one dedicated "Work With Me" page clearly outlining offerings, pricing, and booking process.

- Choose between a "Talk-First" application flow or a "Pay-First" pricing focus.

- Optimize page impact with strong headlines, package naming, and tailored qualification questions.

18

Day 18. Write Your First Blog Post

B ack in 2009, with fingers shaking, I hit publish on my very first blog post. I was fearful of what people would think. Would I get a negative comment? Would anyone like my writing? Do I have any value to add?

That left me with many questions. It was hard enough figuring out how to start a website, but now I had to find a way to share my thoughts consistently.

Would anyone find what I had to say valuable? Was I just contributing to the noise online? Did my message matter?

Maybe you have some of those same fears and doubts. If so, you're in the right place. In this chapter, I have a simple blog post template you can use to write your first post. Follow these four simple steps and launch your blog to the world.

Day 18. Write Your First Blog Post

Most new bloggers make the mistake of using their blog solely as a personal journal or diary. They write post after post about their own thoughts, opinions, and daily events. They do this without asking if this content helps readers.

The result is self-centered writing that may feel therapeutic to the blogger but fails to offer value to anyone else.

The key is to shift the focus from "me" to "them" early on. Before writing each post, reflect on what questions and needs your target audience likely has. Ask yourself the question, "Would my audience search Google to find this post?"

Shape content around being useful first rather than aiming to showcase your own stories or perspectives. As you intentionally serve readers, you will attract an engaged community over time.

Churning out posts just to document your own life may be easy, but it results in shallow content. Readers can sense when a blogger publishes only to indulge themselves rather than to inform or help.

This comes across as self-promotional rather than adding value. The good news is there is a simple four-step formula you can follow to write engaging posts your audience will love.

4-Steps to Writing Your First Blog Post

After working with thousands of new bloggers, I've created a simple 4-step template to help you write your first blog post fast. Those four steps are:

- Step 1. Create a catchy headline

- Step 2. Write the outline before you start writing

- Step 3. Edit your blog post draft

- Step 4. Promote your blog post to the world

Let's take a closer look at each step.

Step 1. Create a Catchy Headline

Post titles are super important for any blogger. Treat them like newspaper headlines. A headline in a newspaper makes or breaks the sale of that paper. Your headline should be catchy and interesting and leave just a bit of curiosity.

When it comes to deciding on a headline, choose one of the following three strategies:

- The magic of list posts

- The power of "how-to" posts

- The blog announcement post

The magic of list posts. It's been proven over time that we love lists. We want to know not only what's on the list but what didn't get included. We click on the headline because we know the article is scannable, and we can see what is included in the list.

Here are a few examples you can use to create your own headline:

- 5 Quick Tips for _____

- 10 Things You Should Never Do When _____

- 5 Ways to _____ (without being pushy)

- 5 great things to do with _____

- 7 ways to be a _____ ninja

- 10 Reasons Not to _____

- 7 _____ Danger Signs

- 7 things _____ Should Never Do

- 21 Secrets the _____ Experts Don't Want You to Know

- 10 _____ Facts You Need to Know

The power of "how-to" posts. Another strategy that will give you tons of blog post ideas is to cover the most important "how-tos" in your niche. Readers love practical posts that lead them to action. It feels like time well spent if I can take concrete action on something I just learned.

A few examples might be:

- How to recover from a _____

- How NOT to get _____

- How to Get _____ in Half the Time

- How to Beat the Fear of _____

- How _____ Will Save You Time, Money, and Stress

- How to clean _____

- How to maintain _____

- How to take care of _____

- How to repair the _____

The blog announcement post. The last strategy I want to share with you is a post you would typically only write once. This post will be a foundational article you will refer back to for years to come.

The two early strategies (list posts and how-to posts) are the formats I use 90% of the time, week in and week out. You're welcome to start with one of them to get your first post published if you would like.

The blog post announcement post is easy enough to write because it doesn't require much guesswork. In a moment, I will share with you a simple writing outline you can use.

As far as a headline, go with something like: "How (name of your blog) Will Help You (insert the goal, promise or purpose of your blog)."

Step 2. Write the Outline Before You Start Writing

Many aspiring bloggers are excited until it's time to sit down and write. Why does it feel like all of my energy and creativity get sucked out about when it's time to write?

Other bloggers say they just wait for inspiration to strike before they sit down to write. If that were true for me, I'd be waiting a long time.

Don't wait till you feel like writing. Most writers I know don't like writing; they like having written. There's a big difference. Never forget the words of Harvard psychologist Jerome Bruner. He said: "You're more likely to act into a feeling than feel into action.'"

If you've successfully accomplished the last step of deciding on a headline, it makes writing much easier. The headline creates the outline for you. Once you've nailed down the outline, all that's left is to fill in the text.

Let's look at how to create an outline from each of our three examples above.

Create an outline for your list post. If you've chosen a list post headline, then you must first decide how many make your list. You can do as few as three or as many as 101. It really comes down to the purpose of the post.

I usually start by opening my writing tool of choice and brainstorming as many examples as I can think of. Once I've created the list, I have my number and my outline. You can also search your topic on Google to look through the topic articles for outline ideas.

Create an outline for your how-to post. If you go with a how-to post, the process will be slightly different. First, start with a beginner's mind. It's easy to skip a few steps because you think they are assumed. We all have the curse of knowledge. We simply forget what it's like to be a beginner.

When outlining a how-to post, you want to think in terms of steps. What's the very first step I should take? Once I complete that step, what's next? Repeat the same process until all of the steps are out of your head and on paper (or screen).

Now, you may end up combining steps, and that's okay. A how-to post will have a minimum of three steps. The maximum number of steps depends on the topic you have chosen.

Create an outline for your blog announcement post. If you chose a blog announcement post, then there is a specific format you should follow.

First, be careful not to make your first blog post only about you. Yes, you will introduce yourself and maybe even share your story. But never forget that your blog is for others. You want to play the role of a guide who helps, serves, or inspires.

The good news is that I already have an outline you should follow. The body of your blog post will include these subheadlines:

- State the goal of your blog

- How this blog will help

- Who you are

The opening of your blog post should state the goal of your blog. Why did you start this blog in the first place? Is there a mission or cause behind your desire to start this blog?

Next, discuss how your blog will benefit the reader. What are some specific ways you plan to help others? Will you publish a weekly blog post? Will you launch a podcast? Will your blog include videos?

Finally, fully introduce yourself and your story. Always remember that you are not the hero of the blog. Your target audience is the hero. You are just the guide. Because of that, we don't lead by touting our credentials or why we are qualified to help.

Still, people will want to know who is behind the blog, so feel free to share your story. But lead with serving and helping first.

Once your outline is ready, just focus on writing a paragraph or two for each point in your outline. Once you do, you have a rough draft ready to go. Now, it's time to edit.

Step 3. Edit Your Blog Post Draft

Blogging is a different way of writing than when you were in English class. It's more conversational, for starters. Also, we break a few of the rules along the way.

Follow this list of basic guidelines, and you'll be a blogging pro in no time:

- Use bullets – My number one tip is to break up your content to make it easy to consume on the computer or mobile device.

- Subheadings – We already covered this in the outline section, but add lots of subheadings

- Short sentences – Keep your sentences short. Enough said.

- Short paragraphs – People scan content when they read online. You want to have two or three sentences per paragraph at most. Make your content easy to scan.

- Relevant Images – Add images to your post to make it more engaging.

- Look for grammar errors – I like to use Grammarly to help me with my grammatical construction.

- Add a call to action – Add ways for readers to join your email list sprinkled throughout your blog posts.

- Publish your post – Get your blog post out to the world! Don't worry about mistakes! You can always come back and fix them later.

Step 4. Promote Your Blog Post to the World

Once your post is live, it's time to share your post with the world. I know this can be a scary feeling when first starting out. My best tip is not to focus on yourself but on how your blog will help others. An ideal place to start is social media. What social media accounts are you already using? Share your blog post there first. Remember, you can do it in a non-pushy way. If you're not sure what to put in your social media post, I have a sample script below you can use:

"Hey friends, I've decided to start a blog with the goal of helping others. I've just published my first post! It would mean the world to me if you would click the link, read this post, and then come back here and share your thoughts with me. Thanks!"

Now, you don't want to bombard your social media newsfeed daily with messages to drive people to your blog post. We want to be helpful, not annoying. You can also enlist some friends to help spread the word. Create a list of 10-20 supportive friends. Be sure this list includes friends and not just acquaintances. Otherwise, this exercise will not work.

Send them a message on Facebook Messenger. Let them know you recently launched a blog and would appreciate it if they shared it on social media. To make this easy for them, you've already typed up a script they can post. It goes like this:

"Hey, guys! My friend Sally, just launched a blog designed to help overwhelmed moms claim back control of their lives. You should check it out here: LINK"

The point of all of this is to get referral traffic to your site. They have friends you don't have. They can reach people you cannot reach.

Day 18 Exercise: Create Your Blog Post Title and Outline

One of the most important skills for bloggers is creating compelling headlines. The title is the first thing readers see and determines whether they'll click through to your content. Identify 3-5 potential blog post topics. Be sure to tailor them to your target audience. These should revolve around common questions or problems faced by people in your niche.

Next, for each identified blog post idea, brainstorm a variety of catchy headlines that would entice your personas to click. Use the headline types covered in this chapter, like "X ways to..." or "How to X without..." as starting points. Create at least 3-4 alternate titles per topic.

After you have headline options for all your post ideas, start an outline for the one headline you feel most excited about. Identify 3-5 pieces of practical advice, steps, or key information you could provide readers under that headline. Resist the urge to start writing sentences - just use bullet points of value you'd share.

Spend the last minute reviewing your outline. Ask yourself, "Will this be a helpful piece of content for the reader?" Remember to always view your content through the lens of reader personas rather than writing for yourself.

Day 18 Key Takeaways:

- Resist the urge to publish blog posts too quickly at first. Build writing skills and audience understanding before ramping up frequency.

- Shape content around serving a specific reader persona. Don't just document your personal thoughts. Reader value must take priority.

- Craft compelling headlines by leveraging proven formulas like "X Ways to..." and "How to X Without..." Headlines determine if readers engage.

19

Day 19. Do a Potential Audience Audit

When Alexander Graham Bell invented the telephone in 1876, he likely didn't foresee the impact it would have on global communication. Within 50 years, over 150 million people worldwide had telephone access. This transformed how humans interacted around the world. Today, many entrepreneurs doubt their ability to find an audience. They have access to technology exponentially more powerful than Bell's telephone.[26]

This chapter will shatter the myth that you have no audience. By adding up your connections across today's digital networks, you will uncover a surprisingly large potential audience for your platform launch. With some diligence and creativity, you can get your message out to hundreds or thousands of people right from your laptop.

Day 19. Do a Potential Audience Audit

Most people assume they have no audience to share their message. Without an email list, social media following, or existing platform, they believe no one will hear what they have to say. This leads to hesitation and self-doubt about launching a website, program, or information product. This keeps people from starting because they assume no one will listen.

However, this belief is flawed when examined more closely. While you may not have a large audience now, you likely have access to far more people than you realize. By leveraging today's digital networks, you can reach people across the globe at scale. The key is to audit your existing connections and contacts methodically.

Why Assuming You Have No Audience is Misguided

We now live in a world of abundant potential contacts. With social media and global interconnectivity, our networks have massively expanded. Over decades of career and life experiences, you likely have hundreds of contacts across various contexts. Dormant connections from your past can be reactivated. New contacts can be made based on shared interests. With some targeted outreach, you can turn these connections into an engaged audience.

Beyond this, your existing contacts have their own networks, too. As we'll discuss later, by sharing your message with your network, it can spread through "word-of-mouth" to entirely new audiences. The takeaway is you have far more potential reach than it appears at first glance. But you need to put in the diligent work of auditing and activating these contacts.

How to Conduct a Potential Audience Audit

Let's walk through a simple 3-step process that will allow us to see the kind of reach we actually have. After you complete this process, you'll be encouraged that you have access to more people than you originally thought. Let's get started.

Step 1. Identify Your Pockets of Online Influence

The first step is to simply identify all the places online where you already have connections. Make a comprehensive list of everywhere you have any type of existing digital reach. Place a checkmark next to any of the following assets you have access to:

- Email List of Subscribers

- Contacts in Your Personal Email

- Personal Facebook Profile (Friend List, Messenger List, and a Facebook Post)

- Facebook Business Page (Formally called Fan Page)

- Facebook Groups You Manage

- YouTube Subscribers

- Instagram Followers

- Snapchat Contacts

- Twitter Followers

- LinkedIn Connections

The key here is to brainstorm and write down all your potential pockets of influence across platforms that can help you reach more people. You likely have more digital access and reach than you think once it's mapped out.

But what if you don't want to feel like you're promoting your business to your friends and families? If you are concerned with this, then let me share a little pro tip for Facebook. Write a Facebook post on your personal profile that asks a simple question and then tag all those who respond.

Let's walk through how this works. If I were a book writing coach, I might publish a Facebook post that says, "Who here has thought about writing a book someday?" I would then add every person who commented to a Facebook friend list labeled "Book Writing Friends." In the future, when I promote my business on my personal Facebook profile, I can publish a post that only gets viewed by my "Book Writing Friends" list.

Over time, you can occasionally publish to your entire friend list and slowly add more targeted friends to your custom friend list. This will allow you to publish more frequently to the segment of your friends who are interested in your topic.

Step 2. Identify Ways to Engage Your Existing Connections

After auditing and identifying all the places with existing digital connections, determine how to engage and reach out to those audiences on each platform. Each social media network and communication channel offers unique messaging options.

You can engage your Facebook connections with posts. You can engage your Instagram connections with Stories and posts. On LinkedIn, you can engage connections through direct messaging. You can engage your email contacts through personalized outreach campaigns. The goal is to determine the best communication method for each media channel.

Step 3. Tally Up Your Total Potential Audience Reach

The final step is to add up all the audience connections you mapped out across platforms into one combined metric. A study by Social Media Today found that the average social media user underestimates their total reach by 75%.

For example, by tallying up your Facebook friends and profiles, LinkedIn networks, email contacts, and more, you may find you have access to hundreds or even thousands more people than you realized.

The key takeaway here is that your total combined potential audience across all digital assets is much greater than any single platform or channel alone. Don't discount all the overlapping networks and unique connections you likely have accumulated.

By doing this entire audience audit process, most people uncover significantly more reach than they ever assumed possible at first. The power comes from compiling all these fragmented pieces together into one unified understanding of your true potential impact.

Day 19 Exercise: Conduct Your Own Potential Audience Audit

Now that you've learned the steps to audit your existing assets and tally up your total audience reach, it's time to put this into practice! Set aside 10-15 minutes to complete the following:

1. Open a blank spreadsheet or document. List out all your existing online profiles, accounts, groups, and digital connections. Cast a wide net, including platforms like personal Facebook profile, Twitter, LinkedIn, email lists & contacts, YouTube, Instagram, Snapchat, TikTok, Facebook Groups, and more.

2. Determine creative ways you could engage each audience. Tailor posts, messages, and campaigns to that platform.

3. Add up all your connections into totals for each section. Then, combine them into a Grand Total Reach Metric.

4. Analyze the results - Which platforms offer you the biggest audience reach? Which could you further cultivate growth and connections? Were you surprised by the total number?

Through this quick exercise, you will understand exactly how many people you truly have the ability to reach online right now. The unlocked potential is there - now start figuring out how to activate it!

Day 19 Key Takeaways:

- You likely have more connections than you assume across digital networks

- Methodically audit all online and offline contacts and communities

- Organize contacts into priority tiers for targeted outreach

- Leverage tools to manage large contact databases for outreach

20

Day 20. Your Social Media Traffic Launch Plan

M y wife and I raced off to Orlando for a quick trip to visit our daughter, who was at a leadership conference.

Our rendezvous point was CityWalk, the vibrant hub just outside Universal Studios. Amidst the crowd's hustle and bustle, something peculiar caught our attention. It was a recurring sight of people clutching pink boxes labeled "VooDoo Donuts."

It seemed like everyone had one, and curiosity got the better of us.

"We need to get our hands on those VooDoo Donuts," we agreed.

Before I knew it, I was also walking around like everyone else with a bright pink box of VooDoo Donuts. This got me thinking about what makes marketing work:

1. Show up often so people see you again and again.

2. Make sure people feel part of something exciting.

3. Get the word out way past just your own words.

In this chapter, I want to teach you how to make your website launch go viral on social media. We are going to tap into the potential audience audit you created in the last chapter. Don't worry; this process is not about trying to sell anyone anything. Instead, we are going to leverage the VooDoo Donuts viral social method.

Day 20. Your Social Media Traffic Launch Plan

Many personal brands sabotage their success when launching a new website. Eager to make a splash, they lead with aggressive sales pitches or talk more about themselves than creating value. These self-defeating strategies yield radio silence.

Rather than making shameless plugs, no one asked for, the most powerful welcome mats meet visitors where they are. This lays the groundwork for nurturing budding loyalty into a loving community.

That's why I guide clients through a 5-day story launch social media series for all new website launches. By sharing the external and internal doubts that paralyze progress, we create a connection with our ideal audience. This vulnerability breeds trust. When we articulate hard-won breakthroughs, it helps others sidestep years of frustrations.

This story-based approach earns attention and opt-ins by putting people first. In this chapter, we will explain the 5-day story launch blueprint in full detail. It will easily bring your ideal audience to your new website.

The 5-Day Story Launch Strategy for Social Media

The 5-Day Story Launch Strategy is a smart approach. It follows Donald Miller's famous framework. Each social media post builds trust and familiarity. It does this by introducing readers to one part of a proven story framework each day for five days. When done right, your daily posts will be like those pink boxes. They bring attention to your message. Let's take a closer look at each post.

Day 1. The External Problem Post

On the first day of the launch, we want to open with the relatable frustrations our clients face. It will quickly connect with the pain they know well. Rather than a "hard sell," we hold up the metaphorical mirror, letting them know, "We see you, and we understand." End the post by sharing how tomorrow we will talk about the internal challenges we face.

Day 2. The Internal Problem Post

The Internal Problem Post shines a light on our doubts and insecurities. We all face these self-limiting beliefs in one way or another. These crippling fears, which breed in isolation, lose power when given a voice. This post should end by letting them know that tomorrow, you'll share why you've decided to act.

Day 3. The Promise Post (Your Big Why)

The Promise Post shares the pivotal backstory that led us to start our new website in the first place. It provides context for why we care so deeply about serving this audience. The post should cover either your before and after story or a client you helped. End the post by sharing how the following day will break down the transformation into steps.

Day 4. The Path Post (Your Core Framework)

The Path Post presents the basics of our strategy. We spell them out from our hard-fought experience. They help readers see how change can happen for them. This manifesto imprints possibility, offering new paths forward. The post should share our 3 to 7 step framework for transformation. End the post, sharing that tomorrow you have a cool free gift to share.

Day 5. The Pitch Post (Your Call to Adventure Invite)

The Pitch Post makes the case for followers or subscribers. It offers an attractive free resource in return for an email registration. This free guide, checklist, or tool with no payment friction makes for an easy "yes" to people joining you on your new journey.

This 5-day social media sequence fosters connection. It does so through struggle and solutions, not through self-promotion like most people do. The goal is relationship before revenue. Trust above transactions. When audiences know beyond a shadow of a doubt that we understand them, they will follow us anywhere.

Day 20 Exercise: Put the 5-Day Story Launch to Work

Now that you've learned the fundamentals of an effective website launch strategy for social media, it's time to make this method work for you. Take out a piece of paper or open your favorite digital notebook. Complete the following exercise:

1. Write down who your ideal audience is. Get very specific - location, gender, age range, interests, etc.

2. Define the external frustration or problem they are facing related to your business services. What outcome do they desire most?

3. Identify the self-limiting doubts and beliefs that hold them back internally from the outcome they want.

4. Craft 2-3 sentences explaining why you are passionate about

helping this audience get past these hurdles to achieve their desired outcome.

5. Outline the core 3-7 step framework or system you use with clients to create success, step by step.

6. Determine what free thing (guide, checklist, etc.) you can give new email subscribers who want to start working with you and your proven framework.

Once done, you will have a custom 5-day social media story. It will launch your new website in an authentic way! Use the templates in this chapter to bring each post to life. Consistency and value are key.

Day 20 Key Takeaways:

- Hook attention with a 5-day story-based social media series.

- Share external and internal struggles people face that are holding them back. Vulnerability builds connection.

- Spotlight your origin story and passion for the cause through a "Big Why" moment. Outline a clear framework that has helped others overcome similar hurdles.

21

Day 21. Your Referral Traffic Launch Plan

"**A** lone, we can do so little; together, we can do so much." This quote by Helen Keller perfectly captures the power of community, especially when launching a new platform. While it's tempting to think we can do everything ourselves, the truth is we all need support. Trying to launch a website or blog solo is not only lonely but inefficient. However, by tapping into our network and recruiting others to help, we can expand our reach exponentially.

In this chapter, we'll explore how to leverage your connections to share your platform launch far and wide. I'll explain why the traditional approach of keeping quiet and hoping for organic growth doesn't work. Instead, I'll share a proven referral launch plan used by top experts to ignite word-of-mouth and quickly build an audience.

Day 21. Your Referral Traffic Launch Plan

Getting support is crucial for launch success. But, many first-timers make missteps that slow progress. Steer clear of these referral launch traps as you build your launch team:

Avoiding Outreach

It's tempting to avoid "bothering" people. But your real friends and connections want to support your big wins! As long as you are considerate in your approach, most will be happy to lend their support. Push past the initial awkwardness for huge launch gains.

No Clear Call to Action

Simply announcing your platform launch without a specific request causes confusion. You need to tell people exactly how to help and promote you. Give advocates ready-made social posts to share. Also, give them usage guidelines. This way, supporting you is totally effortless for them.

Only Reaching Your Niche

Focusing on your core niche is vital for long-term growth. But, sharing widely helps the launch spread. In addition to your niche, also reach out to other circles. They have different interests, backgrounds, and demographics. This will boost awareness.

Not Following Up

Even when people have good intentions, they often forget to follow through on shares and posts. Gently follow up if they previously seemed open to supporting your launch but haven't taken action. A few friendly nudges could make a world of difference amidst the flurry of activity around launching. Don't let their temporary forgetfulness keep your launch from realizing its potential.

By mobilizing your network to share your launch, you gain the power of exponential reach. Not only do their networks see it, but word spreads as their connections interact and share as well. The hardest part is often just asking - most people genuinely want to support your endeavors. Avoid playing it safe and tapping into your community's energy instead. Together, your launch can go from a whimper to a bang.

4 Steps to Recruit Your Launch Team

There are right and wrong ways to recruit your launch team. The good news is your launch team does not have to be your ideal customer avatar. They are connected with thousands of people you aren't. We can leverage their connections to bring awareness to our brand. This is also an easy ask because they are just sharing a link about a new website their friend has launched. There is nothing for sale at this point.

Here are the four steps to recruiting your launch team:

Step 1. Create Your Dream Team List

Make a list of at least 20 potential advocates from your network. Think broadly - friends, family, colleagues, acquaintances. They don't have to be your target audience. Variety helps expand your reach.

Go beyond just the people you interact with regularly. Scroll through your contacts on various platforms like email, social media, and messaging apps to jog your memory. Reach out to old friends, distant relatives, and former colleagues, too. Variety among advocates expands attention as each draws in their own unique circles.

Step 2. Craft Pre-Written Social Media Posts

Craft a pre-written social media post for them to share. Include your name, site topic, and link. Write it from their perspective. Here are two proven posts that can work for any niche:

"My friend [your name] just launched a website about [your topic]. Check it out here: [your URL]."

"Check out this new blog about [your topic] by my friend [your name]. You can find it at [your URL]."

You fill in the brackets with your content and add the links to your site. That way, all your launch team member needs to do is post it on their social media feed.

Also, create 2-3 variations of the post to provide options. Tailor the wording, emojis, images, etc., based on their personal tastes and networks. Make some story-focused and others more promotional. Provide text for platforms like Twitter, Instagram, Facebook, etc.

Step 3. Ask for Their Support

Reach out personally to ask if they'd share the post. Explain you're launching and would appreciate their help spreading the word. Share some insider details about what you're building to get them excited. Communicate the direct benefit to them for supporting your launch goals.

Step 4. Show Gratitude

Thank everyone profusely when they share it! Let them know you appreciate their support. Show gratitude publicly by liking and commenting on their posts. Send a handwritten thank you card to stand out.

Highlight their support on your platform through shares and tags. As a tangible thank you, offer discounts or free access to products.

Bonus. Create a Private Facebook Group for the Launch

If you want to take things to the next level, consider creating a private Facebook group for your launch. You can add everyone who says yes to your request to the group, accelerating communication and interactions. You can even host contests and give away prizes for people who take action and promote your new website.

Day 21 Exercise: Create Your Referral Traffic Launch Plan

To implement these ideas, let's start by making a list of at least 20 potential launch team members you can recruit for your launch team. Then, craft 2-3 social posts they can easily share on their networks.

Consider making posts that will work on many sites, like Facebook, Twitter, and Instagram. Make them enthusiastic but casual, written from their perspective.

Then, personally contact them to ask if they'd be willing to help you spread the word. Follow up if needed, and make sure to express your gratitude when they share it.

Day 21 Key Takeaways:

The key takeaways around launching with referral traffic include:

- Consider creating a launch team to help spread the word about your new site

- Provide clear, pre-written posts for them to share on social media

- Follow up if needed, and thank them profusely for their support

22

The Launch Your Platform 21-Day Action Plan

C ongratulations on completing this journey to launching your own personal brand! You should feel proud of taking this important first step to sharing your message with the world.

It's normal to feel a little nervous as you put yourself out there. Just remember - your message matters. Your experiences can help and inspire others going through similar struggles. We all start unsure of ourselves. But your authentic stories carry power no expert credential alone ever could.

Focus on serving whoever needs your message most. Write from the heart, no matter the size of your audience today. Some of history's most influential works started small before catching fire based on the value they gave.

You now have all the tools needed to overcome common hurdles standing between new messengers like yourself and success. This book equips you to handle platform setup, content creation, marketing, and everything in between. So whenever self-doubt creeps in, recall the guidance these pages contain.

Your dream to impact lives through your writing, coaching, or speaking is absolutely within reach. Our world needs more compassion and wisdom - exactly what you offer. Feel optimistic knowing everything that brought you here has prepared you for what comes next. I applaud you for undertaking this fulfilling yet challenging path. Now go make your unique mark!

If you prefer going through this material with a physical workbook, be sure to check out the Launch Your Platform Companion Workbook. This supplementary guide contains all the exercises from the book in a convenient print format. Completing them with paper and pen can help the lessons stick even more.

Refer back any time you need motivation or want to revisit the core principles that empowered your personal brand launch. Having an offline reference helps many people process, retain, and apply these essential concepts.

You can learn more at PlatformGrowthBooks.com.

So, pick up the workbook if you learn best by writing rather than reading digitally. Either way, you now hold the keys to success!

The Launch Your Platform 21-Day Action Plan

Below, you'll find the complete list of actions I recommend you take to launch your platform online. By taking one action a day over the next 21 days, you'll be on your way to building a profitable personal brand.

- Day 1. Create a Simple Launch Plan Draft

- Day 2. Select Your Primary Brand Voice

- Day 3. Choose the Right Brand Type (Personal vs Private)

- Day 4. Pick Your Domain Name

- Day 5. Select Your Brand Colors

- Day 6. Create Your Brand Logo

- Day 7. Create Your Aspirational Headline

- Day 8. Create The Big 3 Challenges & Success Steps

- Day 9. Design Your Main Call to Action

- Day 10. Craft Your Brand Story Home Page

- Day 11. Choose Your Website Hosting Platform

- Day 12. Create Your First Lead Magnet

- Day 13. Select Your Email List Service

- Day 14. Design the Perfect Landing Page

- Day 15. Set Up Your Automated Prospect Funnel

- Day 16. Create Your About Me Page

- Day 17. Create Your Work with Me Page

- Day 18. Write Your First Blog Post

- Day 19. Do a Potential Audience Audit

- Day 20. Create Your Social Media Traffic Launch Plan

- Day 21. Create Your Referral Traffic Launch Plan

Thank You

I want to express my gratitude for choosing and purchasing my book. In a world overflowing with choices, you selected mine, and for that, I'm truly thankful.

Before we part ways, may I request a minor favor? Would it be too much to ask for you to leave a review on the platform? For an independent author like myself, receiving direct reader feedback through reviews significantly contributes to the success of the work.

Your insights will guide me in creating content that effectively aids you in achieving your desired results. Your feedback is highly valuable to me. Thank you for your time and consideration.

Leave a review by going to: **JMill.Biz/launch-review**

23
What's Next?

Y ou might be wondering, "What's next?" Once your platform is launched, where should you put your time and attention?

Whenever my private clients ask this question, I usually reply, "We need to validate your offer!"

In other words, what's the easiest and fastest way to get something up for sale?

I like to look for low-hanging fruit opportunities. I call these opportunities validation offers. To qualify as a validation offer, they must be:

- Easy to create without complex funnels or technology

- Ability to get paid before we spend too much time on it

- Delivers quick feedback so we can speed up the learning curve

- Validate our market and that we are going in the right direction

- Give us confidence that we can build this business

There are four offers that check off all of the boxes above for me. Those offers are:

- Validation Offer 1. Writing a short Amazon Kindle Book

- Validation Offer 2. Launching a Mini-Course

- Validation Offer 3. Hosting a Paid Virtual Workshop

- Validation Offer 4. Creating a 4-Week Group Coaching Program

Want to know the step-by-step playbook on how to launch these validation offers? That's what book three in the series is all about.

The book is called *Validate Your Offer: A 28-Day Profit Plan to Test the Market First and Turn Ideas into Income as a Writer, Coach, Teacher, or Speaker.*

Grab your copy today by going to: PlatformGrowthBooks.com

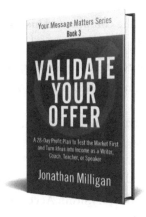

1. Interesting Engineering. "YouTube's History and Its Impact on the Internet." Interesting Engineering, 26 Jan. 2023, https://interestingengineering.com/culture/youtubes-history-and-its-impact-on-the-internet. Accessed 26 Jan. 2024.

2. "The Estée Story." EL Companies, https://www.elcompanies.com/en/who-we-are/the-lauder-family/the-estee-story. Accessed 26 Jan. 2024.

3. Demontis, Uta. "When You Speak To Everyone You Speak to No One." Website Design for Coaches, https://websitedesignforcoaches.com/when-you-speak-to-everyone/. Accessed 26 Jan. 2024.

4. O'Neill, Conor. "Understanding Personality: The 12 Jungian Archetypes." Conor Neill, 21 Apr. 2018, https://conorneill.com/2018/04/21/understanding-personality-the-12-jungian-archetypes/. Accessed 26 Jan. 2024.

5. Morga, Adriana. "The complicated history of P.T. Barnum: How CT helped make the circus king." CTInsider, CTInsider, 16 June 2021, https://www.ctinsider.com/living/article/Ringling-brothers-circus-pt-barnum-ct-17182072.php. Accessed 31 Jan. 2024.

6. Brown, Brené. "About." Brené Brown, 2022, https://brenebrown.com/about/. Accessed 31 Jan. 2024.

7. "History." Honda UK, Honda, https://www.honda.co.uk/cars/world-of-honda/past/history.html. Accessed 31 Jan. 2024.

8. "The Birth of Ford Motor Company." The Ford Story | The Henry Ford, The Henry Ford, https://hfha.org/the-ford-story/the-birth-of-ford-motor-company/. Accessed 31 Jan. 2024.

9. Mancini, Jeannine. "Jeff Bezos Wanted Amazon Named 'Rele ntless.com' Because It Reflected the Scale of His Ambitions." Yahoo! Finance, Yahoo!, 28 Jan. 2024, finance.yahoo.com/new s/jeff-bezos-wanted-amazon-named-184721277.html. Accessed 31 Jan. 2024.

10. Rising Above The Noise. https://www.risingabovethenoise.co m/. Accessed 31 Jan. 2024.

11. Namecheap. Namecheap, 2023, www.namecheap.com/. Ac cessed 31 Jan. 2024.

12. "NRG eSports sued over attempt to trademark 'NRG'." Sports Business Journal, 2 Aug. 2022, https://www.sportsbusinessjournal.com/Esports/Sections/Legal -and-Governance/2022/08/NRG-trademark-lawsuit.aspx. Accessed 31 Jan. 2024.

13. "The Story Behind the Subway Logo and Its Meaning." Free Logo Design, 3 July 2020, https://www.freelogodesign.org/blog/2020/07/03/the-stor y-behind-the-subway-logo-and-its-meaning. Accessed 31 Jan. 2024.

14. Our Heart Livery." Southwest50, Southwest Airlines, https://s outhwest50.com/our-stories/our-heart-livery/. Accessed 31 Jan. 2024.

15. "A Diamond Is Forever." De Beers Group, https://www.debe ersgroup.com/about-us/a-diamond-is-forever. Accessed 31 Jan. 2024.

16. Williams, Marlena. "The Little-Known History of the 'Got Milk?' Ad Campaign." Sentient Media, 15 Nov. 2022, https:// sentientmedia.org/milk-ad-history/. Accessed 31 Jan. 2024.

17. Library of Congress. "Fireside Chats of Franklin D. Roosevelt." Library of Congress, https://www.loc.gov/static/programs/national-recording-preservation-board/documents/FiresideChats.pdf. Accessed 31 Jan. 2024.

18. "Wii would like to play." Nintendo, https://nintendo.fandom.com/wiki/Wii_would_like_to_play. Accessed 31 Jan. 2024.

19. "Donald Miller Storybrand Website." Agency Boon, https://www.agencyboon.com/blog/donald-miller-storybrand-website/. Accessed 31 Jan. 2024.

20. "History of Shredded Wheat." I Love Shredded Wheat, http://iloveshreddedwheat.com/history-of-shredded-wheat/. Accessed 31 Jan. 2024.

21. "Yesmail Must Pay $50,000 Penalty to Settle CAN-SPAM Complaint." Chief Marketer, 9 May 2019, https://www.chiefmarketer.com/yesmail-must-pay-50000-penalty-to-settle-can-spam-complaint/. Accessed 31 Jan. 2024.

22. Ransom, Diana. "How YouTube Crashed Our Website." Inc.com, Inc., 17 June 2015, https://www.inc.com/magazine/201507/diana-ransom/how-youtube-crashed-our-website.html. Accessed 31 Jan. 2024.

23. "McDonald's." Encyclopædia Britannica, https://www.britannica.com/topic/McDonalds. Accessed 31 Jan. 2024.

24. Library of Congress. "Autobiography." Finding Benjamin Franklin | Research Guides, Library of Congress, https://guides.loc.gov/finding-benjamin-franklin/autobiographyAccessed 31 Jan. 2024.

25. https://www.arca.com/resources/apples-genius-bar/

26. The Franklin Institute. "The Story Behind the Telephone." The Franklin Institute Science Museum, https://fi.edu/en/blog/story-behind-telephone. Accessed 31 Jan. 2024.

Made in United States
Troutdale, OR
12/09/2024

25897566R00106